Health Targets in Europe

The European Observatory on Health Systems and Policies supports and promotes evidence-based health policy-making through comprehensive and rigorous analysis of health systems in Europe. It brings together a wide range of policy-makers, academics and practitioners to analyse trends in health reform, drawing on experience from across Europe to illuminate policy issues.

The European Observatory on Health Systems and Policies is a partnership between the World Health Organization Regional Office for Europe, the Governments of Belgium, Finland, Greece, Norway, Slovenia, Spain and Sweden, the Veneto Region of Italy, the European Investment Bank, the Open Society Institute, the World Bank, the London School of Economics and Political Science and the London School of Hygiene & Tropical Medicine.

Health Targets in Europe

Learning from experience

Edited by
Matthias Wismar
Martin McKee
Kelly Ernst
Divya Srivastava
Reinhard Busse

European
Observatory
on Health Systems and Policies

Keywords:
HEALTH POLICY
HEALTH PRIORITIES
STRATEGIC PLANNING
HEALTH STATUS INDICATORS
DELIVERY OF HEALTH CARE - organization and administration
PROGRAM EVALUATION - methods
EUROPE

ISBN 978 92 890 4284 0

Printed and bound in the European Union

Contents

Foreword   vii

Acknowledgements   ix

Chapter 1 Introduction   1
   Matthias Wismar, Martin McKee, Kelly Ernst, Divya Srivastava, Reinhard Busse

PART 1: HEALTH TARGETS: CONCEPTS AND PRINCIPLES   7

Chapter 2 The Emergence of Health Targets: Some Basic Principles   9
   Divya Srivastava, Martin McKee

Chapter 3 On target? Monitoring and Evaluation   23
   Martin McKee

Chapter 4 Improving the Effectiveness of Health Targets   41
   Kelly Ernst, Matthias Wismar, Reinhard Busse, Martin McKee

PART 2: COUNTRY AND REGION EXPERIENCES   51

Chapter 5 Catalonia: Improved Intelligence and Accountability?   53
   Ricard Tresserras, Pilar Brugulat

Chapter 6 England: Intended and Unintended effects   63
   Peter C. Smith

Chapter 7 Flanders: Health Targets as a Catalyst for Action   83
Stephan Van den Broucke

Chapter 8 France: Targeting Investment in Health   101
Valérie Paris, Dominique Polton

Chapter 9 Germany: Targets in a Federal System   123
Matthias Wismar, Barbara Philippi, Hildegard Klus

Chapter 10 Hungary: Targets Driving Improved Health Intelligence 137
Zoltán Vokó, Róza Ádány

**Chapter 11 The Russian Federation: Difficult History of
Target Setting**   147
Kirill Danishevski

Foreword

The World Health Organization and its Regional Office for Europe in particular has a longstanding and productive experience with the use of targets in support of implementation and monitoring of its Health for All (HFA) policy. The last HFA update in 2005 encourages countries to set national targets as key governance tools that can help them in implementing their own health policies. The HFA update, however, did not include any normative targets for the whole European Region. Experience has shown that in some instances setting common targets for all countries in the Region is artificial, unfair or even misleading. National targets are much better at taking into account the economic, social and political diversity which characterizes our Region and at including the specific needs and priorities of individual countries.

The need to improve health systems stewardship was at the core of the discussions of the recent WHO European Ministerial Conference on Health Systems "Health Systems, Health and Wealth" which took place in Tallinn, Estonia, in June 2008. The Conference discussions, its publications and the Tallinn Charter, endorsed by all our Member States, make a strong case for investing in health systems. Well-functioning health systems have a major impact on health and thus a significant contribution to economic growth and overall societal well-being. The key is how do we ensure that health systems function well or, in other words, how do we improve the performance of health systems? The review of the experience in the Conference clearly shows that the ability of health authorities to exercise stewardship and governance is key in securing improved health systems performance.

As this volume shows, targets, when designed and applied appropriately, constitute an effective governance tool at national, sub-national and local levels. They can help to define policies and set priorities, involve stakeholders and build consensus, guide the collection of intelligence and evaluation, develop legislation and incentives and guide the allocation of funds and purchase of services. Health targets can be particularly instrumental in supporting policies that go beyond the health care services on to other key sectors addressing the broader socioeconomic determinants of health.

This book is therefore very much welcomed as it will help to expand our knowledge on the strengths and limitations of targets. It can assist policy-makers to better understand what it takes to set targets adequately, how to embed them within health strategies and how best to link them with other governance tools and strategies. The book will also be instrumental in achieving a better understanding of the contextual factors conducive to the successful use of health targets. WHO, together with the other partners of the Observatory, is thus happy to present this volume which will make an important contribution to the arsenal of evidence to improve the governance of health systems.

Dr Nata Menabde
Deputy Regional Director
WHO Regional Office for Europe

August 2008

Acknowledgements

We are grateful for the generous contributions made to this project by numerous individuals and organizations. In particular, we are heavily indebted to our chapter authors whose commitment of both time and knowledge made this study possible.

We would like to thank Merck and Co., Inc., Whitehouse Station, NJ, United States of America[1], for providing the funding for this project. Without their assistance, this research would not have been possible. In particular, we would like to express our gratitude to Dr Jeffrey Sturchio (Vice President, Corporate Responsibility) and Ms Melinda Hanisch (Manager, European Public Affairs) for their endless support, encouragement and confidence in this project.

We have greatly benefited from presenting progress and preliminary results of the project to the MSD Academic Advisory Board on Health Policy Innovation. In particular we would like to thank the chairpersons Marshal Marinker and Ilona Kickbusch. Workshop participants provided valuable comments on preliminary results and case studies presented at meetings including conferences on poverty and health (Armut und Gesundheit) in Berlin (Germany) 2007; at the Styrian health conference (Austria) 2007; and the European Health Forum Gastein (Austria) 2006.

Summaries of early drafts of the chapters were published in *Euro Observer* 2006 Vol. 8 No. 1. Individual chapters were reviewed by Sibylle Angele (GVG) and Josep Figueras (European Observatory on Health Systems and Policies). The book was presented as a draft for comment at the WHO European Ministerial Conference on Health Systems held in Tallinn, Estonia, 25-27 June 2008.

---

[1] Merck & Co., Inc. operates in most countries outside North America as Merck Sharp & Dohme, or MSD.

Many thanks to the European Observatory on Health Systems and Policies team in Brussels for their support throughout the project. Additionally, this book would not have been possible without the hard work of the publication team, in particular Jonathan North, Caroline White, Jo Woodhead and David Gibbons.

List of Contributors

Róza Ádány – Professor of Public Health and Director of the School of Public Health, University of Debrecen, Hungary.

Pilar Brugulat – Department of Health and Social Security of Catalonia, Barcelona, Spain.

Reinhard Busse – Professor of Health Management, Technische Universität Berlin; Associate Head of Research Policy and Head of the Berlin hub, European Observatory on Health Systems and Policies.

Kirill Danishevski – Associate Professor at the IM Sechenov Moscow Medical Academy. Previously, Research Fellow at the London School of Hygiene & Tropical Medicine (LSHTM) and Public Health Consultant, Open Health Institute, Moscow, Russian Federation.

Kelly Ernst – freelance technical officer, European Observatory on Health Systems and Policies.

Hildegard Klus – Association for Social Security Policy and Research (GVG), Bonn, Germany.

Martin McKee – Professor of European Public Health and co-director of the European Centre on Health of Societies in Transition (ECOHOST), LSHTM; Head of Research Policy and Head of the London hub, European Observatory on Health Systems and Policies.

Valérie Paris – economist, Organisation for Economic Co-operation and Development (OECD), Paris, France. Previously at ECOHOST.

Barbara Philippi – economist, Federal Ministry of Health, Germany. Formerly, at the Association for Social Security Policy and Research (GVG).

Dominique Polton – Director of Strategy and Statistical Studies, Caisse Nationale de l'Assurance Maladie des Travailleurs Salariés (CNAMTS), France.

Peter C Smith – Professor of Economics and Director of the Centre for Health Economics, University of York, United Kingdom.

Divya Srivastava – PhD student in pharmaceutical policy, London School of Economics and Political Science (LSE). Formerly, technical officer, European Observatory on Health Systems and Policies.

Ricard Tresserras – Deputy Director for Health Planning, Department of Health and Social Security of Catalonia, Barcelona, Spain.

Stephan Van den Broucke, PhD – Research Group for Health Psychology, KU Leuven, Belgium. Presently Executive Agency for Health and Consumers, European Commission, Luxembourg.

Zoltán Vokó – Assistant Professor and Course Director of the MSc in Epidemiology, School of Public Health, University of Debrecen, Hungary.

Matthias Wismar – Senior Health Policy Analyst, European Observatory on Health Systems and Policies.

Chapter 1
Introduction

Matthias Wismar, Martin McKee, Kelly Ernst, Divya Srivastava,
Reinhard Busse

What is this health system (or policy) seeking to achieve? This is a simple question at one level but highly complex at another. The simple answer is often along the lines of – to make people better or (with a little more sophistication) to achieve the maximum possible health gain; respond to the legitimate expectations of those it serves; and raise the necessary resources equitably. The complex answer requires mechanisms to ascertain whether it is actually doing any of these things. Yet, even in some of the richest countries, those responsible for many health systems often have not even begun to set out what they are seeking to achieve, how it might be monitored and what they will do if performance falls short of expectations.

This book looks at the phenomena that have been termed (with some variations) health targets. It seeks to understand their uses and abuses by drawing on the experiences of a number of European countries in which they have been implemented in various ways. It explores the methodological issues involved in setting and monitoring targets and the political issues that arise when using them.

Self-evidently, a target is something which one aims to hit. In other words, an explicit commitment to achieve specified results within a defined time. A target may be quantitative (e.g. increasing the immunization rate by x%) or qualitative (e.g. introduction of a national screening programme). It may involve a change in outcomes (e.g. reduction in mortality) or in processes (e.g. percentage of a population that takes up invitations to screening tests). An ideal target is said to be SMART – specific (to the ultimate health goal to be pursued), measurable (able to be monitored with data that either exist or can be collected), accurate (in order to know whether the target has been hit), realistic (challenging but actually achievable) and time bound (time taken to achieve the target should be specified).

Targets can be set at any level. Individuals may set targets for themselves during their annual appraisals. A health facility may set targets to be achieved over the forthcoming year (such as a reduction in infection rates) and specialized units may set their own targets within the facility. However, this book focuses on the experience of setting health targets at the political level, by those responsible for health policy in regions, countries and international bodies.

Clearly, target setting is not new. Military leaders have set targets from the dawn of recorded history, for example to capture a city or defeat an enemy army. While not minimizing the complexity involved in achieving the objective in practice, in such circumstances the overall task and the means of doing it are relatively straightforward. Military leaders have forces at their disposal that can be deployed on their orders, with the expectation that they will obey even if their lives are at risk from doing so. Indeed, experience shows that military-political objectives that are anything but SMART often lead to disaster.

Inevitably, health policy-makers face more complex scenarios. The initial situation is often unknown, with only the most basic information about the health needs of the population concerned. The resources available are often unclear as those who deliver health care have their own, often competing, objectives. Perhaps unsurprisingly, the easiest course is to continue what is already being done while hoping that somehow the system will respond to changing circumstances.

This may be the most appropriate course of action. Health care is extremely complex and those working at the regional or national level cannot possibly synthesize the vast amount of information accumulated by individual health professionals. The experience of the Soviet Union does not offer encouragement to those who advocate central planning. Equally, it is clear that individual health professionals do not have all the information. They know about those who seek their care but little or nothing about those whose needs are unmet. The increasing ethnic and linguistic heterogeneity of many societies makes it possible that the needs of entire sections of populations may be unrecognized. Health professionals working alone may also find it difficult to put in place the complex packages of care that increasingly are required to respond to the needs of ageing populations with multiple complex disorders. Similarly, an individual who sees some rare diseases only every few years will not be well-placed to ascertain whether such diseases are becoming more or less common.

For these reasons, there is an argument that the clinical decisions of individual practitioners and organizational decisions made by managers of individual facilities should be embedded within a larger system that can determine the actual health needs of the overall population, what should be put in place to meet them and whether they are being met.

More recently, an additional level of complexity has emerged. Growing recognition of the many determinants of health that lie outside the formal health system has stimulated multisectoral policies to improve health. This involves engagement with policies in sectors as diverse as agriculture, food policy, the environment, housing, transport and the workplace (Ståhl et al., 2006). Notable recent examples of the political commitment to this approach include the Council Conclusion of the Finnish European Union Presidency (Council of the European Union 2006) and the declaration endorsed by European Union (EU) governments, the European Commission and the World Health Organization (WHO) following a recent conference hosted by the Italian Health Ministry (Ministry of Health, Italy 2007).

To add to the complexity, health policy in federal countries may be devolved to regional or other subnational administrations. Countries in which one or more regions have employed targets include Australia, Belgium, Canada, Germany (Gesellschaft für Versicherungswissenschaft und -gestaltung (GVG) e v 2007), the Russian Federation, Spain, Sweden, Switzerland, the United Kingdom of Great Britain and Northern Ireland (Northern Ireland Department of Health Social Services and Personal Safety 2002; Secretary of State for Health 1999; Welsh Assembly Government 2002) and the United States of America.

This book builds on a substantial body of work already undertaken to study health targets, both in Europe and elsewhere (Busse and Wismar 2002; Claveranne and Teil 2003; Ritsatakis et al. 2000; van de Water and van Herten 1998). A WHO review reported that 41 out of the then 52 Member States of WHO's European Region had either adopted or drafted policies which included health targets (WHO Regional Office for Europe 2005), although their nature and implementation varied widely. Targets have also been used in health policies outside Europe, in Australia (Commonwealth Department of Human Services and Health 1994) Canada (Williamson et al. 2003), Japan (Ministry of Health and Welfare 2000), Republic of Korea, New Zealand (Signal and Durham 2000; Wise and Nutbeam 1999) and the United States of America (US Department of Health and Human Services 1991; US Department of Health and Human Services 2000).

Despite the scale of this activity, there is scant evidence of the effectiveness of health targets. The process of establishing targets may have little linkage with mechanisms for governing, financing and delivering health services (Wismar and Busse 2002). For example, the English target-driven health policy, Health of the Nation (Department of Health 1992), produced only limited changes in the use of resources. Some, such as those related to mental health, lacked credibility among those responsible for achieving them (London School of Hygiene & Tropical Medicine 1998; McKee and Fulop 2000; Universities of Leeds and Glamorgan and London School of Hygiene & Tropical Medicine 1998). A recent analysis of Swedish public health targets concluded that they were not sufficiently explicit to be used in governing the health system (Lager et al. 2007). Health targets may even be counterproductive – the current debate on their use is dominated by examples from the English National Health Service (NHS) in which the use of numerous extremely detailed targets, backed by incentives and sanctions, has led to widespread opportunistic behaviour. Distortion and even misreporting of data, accompanied by adoption of dysfunctional actions, achieve the targets but worsen patients' situations (Wismar et al. 2006).

Given the gap between the widespread use of health targets and the evidence for their effectiveness, and in a situation where there are growing demands for effective governance mechanisms within health systems, it is timely to assess the experiences of those countries that have employed targets. This book draws on a series of case studies (based on a standard analytical framework) written by experts from the countries concerned, to consider what has worked and what has not.

Part 1 brings together the key concepts, principles and results of the cross-sectional analysis. Chapter 2 sets the scene for the overall book, examining the rationale for governments to devise health strategies and use targets to express what they hope to achieve. It contains a brief review of some basic requirements for target definition and implementation and some initial conclusions. Chapter 3 is an examination of the main technical issues involved in target setting. Chapter 4 is a consideration of the lessons emerging from experiences with health targets.

Part 2 of the book brings together case studies from seven countries or subnational entities: Catalonia (Spain), England (United Kingdom), Flanders (Belgium), France, Germany, Hungary and the Russian Federation. Some focus on health services, others deal with health promotion and/or health determinants.

REFERENCES

Busse R, Wismar M (2002). Health target programmes and health care services – any link? A conceptual and comparative study (part 1). *Health Policy,* 59(3):209-221.

Claveranne J-P, Teil A (2003). *Les modalités de définition des objectifs et strategies de santé. Description et analyse de dispositifs des pays de l'Union Europeenne et d'Amerique du Nord. Tome II, descriptions verticales.* Lyon, France, GRAPHOS-CNRS.

Commonwealth Department of Human Services and Health (1994). *Better health outcomes for Australians. National goals, targets and strategies for better health outcomes into the next century.* Canberra, Australian Government Publishing Service.

Council of the European Union (2006). *Council conclusions on Health in All Policies (HiAP) (EPSCO).* Brussels, Council of the European Union.

Department of Health (1992). *The Health of the Nation: a strategy for health in England.* London, The Stationery Office.

Gesellschaft für Versicherungswissenschaft und -gestaltung (GVG) e v (2007). *Gesundheitsziele im Föderalismus: Programme der Länder und des Bundes.* Bonn, Nanos Verlag oHG.

Lager A, Guldbrandsson K, Fossum B (2007). The chance of Sweden's public health targets making a difference. *Health Policy,* 80(3):413-421.

London School of Hygiene & Tropical Medicine (1998). Evaluation of the implementation of the Health of the Nation. In: *Universities of Leeds and Glamorgan and the London School of Hygiene & Tropical Medicine. The Health of the Nation - a policy assessed. A report commissioned by the Department of Health.* London, The Stationery Office:69-182.

McKee M, Fulop N (2000). On target for health? Health targets may be valuable, but context is all important. *BMJ,* 320(7231):327-328.

Ministry of Health, Italy. (2007). *Declaration on Health in All Policies.* Rome, Ministry of Health.

Ministry of Health and Welfare (2000). *Healthy Japan 21.* Tokyo, Ministry of Health and Welfare.

Northern Ireland Department of Health, Social Services and Personal Safety (2002). *Investing in health.* Belfast, Northern Ireland Department of Health, Social Services and Personal Safety.

Ritsatakis A et al. (2000). *Exploring health policy development in Europe.* Copenhagen, WHO Regional Office for Europe.

Secretary of State for Health (1999). *Saving lives: our healthier nation.* London, The Stationery Office.

Signal L, Durham G (2000). A case study of health goals in New Zealand. *Australian and New Zealand Journal of Public Health,* 24(2):192-197.

Ståhl T et al. (2006). *Health in all policies: prospects and potentials.* Helsinki, Finland, Ministry of Social Affairs and Health, Health Department.

US Department of Health and Human Services (1991). *Healthy People 2000: national health promotion and disease prevention objectives.* Washington DC, US Department of Health and Human Services.

US Department of Health and Human Services (2000). *Healthy People 2010.* Washington DC, US Government Printing Office.

Universities of Leeds and Glamorgan and London School of Hygiene & Tropical Medicine (1998). *The Health of the Nation - a policy assessed. Two reports commissioned for the Department of Health.* London, The Stationery Office.

van de Water HPA, van Herten LM (1998). *Health policies on target? Review of health target and priority setting in 18 European countries.* Leiden, TNO.

Welsh Assembly Government (2002). *Targeting health improvement for all: a consultation document.* Cardiff, Welsh Assembly Government, Health Promotion Division.

Williamson DL et al. (2003). Implementation of provincial/territorial health goals in Canada. *Health Policy,* 64(2):173-191.

Wise M, Nutbeam D (1999). Public health and disease prevention – moving forward in New Zealand and Australia: the role of policy in health promotion – an international perspective from Australia. *Healthcare Review - Online,* 3:9.

Wismar M, Busse R (2002). Outcome-related health targets – political strategies for better health outcomes: a conceptual and comparative study (part 2). *Health Policy,* 59(3):223-241.

Wismar M et al. (2006). Health targets and (good) governance. *EuroObserver,* 8(Spring):1-8.

WHO Regional Office for Europe (2005). *The Health for All policy framework for the WHO European Region: Regional Committee for Europe, Bucharest, 12-15 September 2005. Fifty-fifth session.* Copenhagen, WHO Regional Office for Europe (http://www.euro.who.int/Document/RC55/edoc08.pdf, accessed 6 May 2008).

Part 1

Health Targets: Concepts and Principles

Chapter 2

The Emergence of Health Targets: Some Basic Principles

Divya Srivastava, Martin McKee

Introduction

Targets are no more and no less than a means to an end (Marinker, 2002). They indicate where one is aiming to be and thus can be used to decide how to get there. However, this makes a very large assumption – that society, acting through governments or other bodies with an interest in health care (such as sickness funds or health-care providers), has articulated where it wants to be in terms of health. This should not be taken for granted. Governments have many targets, typically expressed in economic terms such as economic growth, control of inflation rates or public sector borrowing; or in the accumulation of physical capital such as houses or roads built. Rarely are their goals expressed in terms of the health of their populations. Thus, to begin this book, it is useful to reflect on why the state has a legitimate role in promoting health rather than simply leaving it to individuals to act.

The argument for health strategies

All European countries have a health system. Yet what is a health system for? What do we expect it to do and how can we know if it has been done? Until recently, few people asked these superficially simple questions. Rather, it was assumed that a health system's role was to exist – to be there when needed. Health systems were seen as meeting the needs of many individuals, each with their own health needs and expectations. Hopefully there would be a beneficial encounter between an individual and the system but, apart from the individual concerned and his or her friends and family, no one had any practical interest in the result. Health care was provided to those who asked (and, in some cases, could pay), with little regard for those who did not express their needs as demand. It was assumed that the health-care provider would act in good faith to provide care that was effective, but no one ever checked.

The obvious weaknesses in this approach probably did not matter very much when health care had little to offer. This was the case until at least the end of the nineteenth century when the introduction of safe anaesthesia and asepsis made surgery (especially that involving the opening of body cavities) more likely to cure than to kill. Hence, the number of people in a population who would voluntarily subject themselves to surgery (and health-care's impact on population health) was limited. By the 1960s, the situation had changed out of all recognition. New pharmaceutical products were becoming available that made it possible to treat large numbers of people with common chronic disorders, in particular hypertension, as well as less common conditions such as cancers. Sulphonamides and penicillins were joined by new classes of antibiotics that could treat many common infections, at least for a time. Modern health-care's scope to improve population health was greater than it had ever been (Nolte and McKee 2004).

Yet evidence slowly emerged that health care was not achieving its full potential. Even in systems providing universal access to care, many of those who might benefit from treatment were not doing so. At the same time, it was being realized that some of the health care provided was ineffective (Cochrane 1972). Of course, these were concerns for the individuals affected but, increasingly, they were also seen as a concern for society. It is true that society has always taken an interest in whether some people receive effective health care. City authorities in many countries had put in place mechanisms to look after those with infectious diseases (such as tuberculosis) or mental disorders, especially where those affected were potentially violent or disruptive. Although these policies may have owed something to altruism, society's main reason to act was to protect its members from either contagion or physical attack. However, in some places, society began to take an interest in populations by asking whether the health system it had put in place was delivering what was intended.

A similar evolution has taken place in the broader determinants of health. Again, it has always been accepted that society should take action on health in some circumstances, classically infectious disease and mental health. Fundamentally, this was to protect the interests of elites. Infectious diseases posed a personal risk to those in power, especially once mass urbanization began in the nineteenth century. The rich were no longer able to maintain large physical distances from the poor but were forced to breathe the same air and drink the same water, thus rendering themselves susceptible to the same diseases. The state also had an interest in promoting health as a means of protecting itself from attack. Thus, in countries such as France and the United

Kingdom, major public health initiatives arose in response to the realization that there were not enough young men to supply the armies; those who were available were not sufficiently healthy to do anything useful. In due course, this concern moved beyond the need for a large and effective military force to a concern about the entire workforce's ability to contribute to the economic development of a country. This instigated a series of policies that, in Europe, led progressively to universal education, health care and/or health insurance and the widespread provision of social housing. More recently, these ideas have been developed within a growing literature demonstrating how better population health feeds into economic growth (Suhrcke et al. 2006) – healthier people are more likely to participate, and remain, in the workforce and to achieve higher levels of productivity.

Yet, even when it is accepted that the state has a legitimate role in promoting the health of its population, it is still important to ask where the limits of its responsibility lie. When is the state justified in acting to constrain or otherwise influence individuals' choices? This is an extremely complex question that goes far beyond what can be covered in this book (McKee and Colagiuri 2007). However, it is important to consider some key principles.

First, many unhealthy choices are not made freely. In many countries, people on low incomes simply cannot eat healthily, primarily because they cannot afford more expensive foods such as fresh fruit and vegetables. Their situation is often exacerbated because large retailers build their stores in wealthier locations, recognizing the limited scope for sales in deprived areas. Poor people would incur high transport costs and must depend on small convenience stores selling mainly preserved food at comparatively high prices. Similarly, people face problems with access even when a health service (such as a screening programme) is made freely available. Those on low incomes particularly are constrained by distance and travel costs or, in the case of migrants, because information is not available in a language they understand.

Second, there is a consensus that it is appropriate for the state to intervene when one person's action causes harm to others. This was conceded by John Stuart Mill, whose writings provide the intellectual basis for libertarianism.

> …the sole end for which mankind are warranted, individually or collectively, in interfering with the liberty of action of any of their number is self-protection. That the only purpose for which power can be rightfully exercised over any member of a civilised community, against his will, is to prevent harm to others. His own good, either physical or moral, is not a sufficient warrant. He cannot rightfully be compelled to do or forbear because it will be better for him to do so, because it will

make him happier, because, in the opinion of others, to do so would be wise, or even right. (Mill 2003).

Yet even Mill conceded that there were certain limits to an individual's right to organize his or her own life, such as the need for a prohibition on selling oneself into slavery. However, beyond the obvious (e.g. a state law enforcement agencies' right to take direct action to stop someone opening fire on the public), in what circumstances is the risk to others sufficient to provoke action?

Ultimately, almost every action undertaken by anyone will have (good or bad) consequences for someone else. Norms vary between countries and change over time. In the nineteenth century, the United Kingdom was willing to go to war against China to secure the right to export opium; in the twentieth century the British navy patrolled the Caribbean to prevent Colombian cocaine dealers engaging in the same activity. In some cases norms change as the result of new evidence. Thus, the bans on smoking in public places that are now spreading rapidly in many parts of the world are due, at least in part, to the knowledge that second-hand smoke (particularly from cigarettes smouldering in ashtrays) is far more toxic than was previously thought. This fact has been long known to the tobacco industry but actively concealed by them (Diethelm et al. 2005). In other cases, shifts are a result of ideology. During the twentieth century there were concerns about injuries and deaths among motorcycle riders and the subsequent costs incurred by society and the families of those injured. These stimulated legislators in many parts of the world to enact laws requiring the wearing of crash helmets but the prevailing libertarian ideology in some American states led them to revoke existing legislation in the late 1990s. It is assumed that the legislators felt that the significant increases in fatalities (Houston and Richardson 2007) were a cost worth bearing for the right to drive at speed without the encumbrance of a helmet.

Third, there is now an unprecedented amount of evidence on the contributions that different diseases and risk factors make to the overall burden of disease, most obviously as a result of the work of the Global Burden of Disease programme (Ezzati et al. 2004). This highlights the cost of failing to address this avoidable loss of human life. It has also highlighted the inconsistencies in policies that focus on phenomena that cause small numbers of deaths while ignoring some of the main killers. This is exemplified by the events in New York and Washington on 11 September 2001 that caused almost 3000 deaths and gave rise to an unprecedented political response, including the American-led invasion of Afghanistan and the suspension of fundamental legal principles such as habeas corpus. In contrast, firearms are used in the murder of over 9000 American citizens every year but this has not produced legislation to control access to guns. Equally, the avoidable deaths of many thousands of American citizens caused by inadequate access to health care has failed to bring about universal access (Nolte and McKee 2008).

Fourth, there is a growing acceptance that when the state does act, it should ensure that its actions have a prospect of working – policies should be based on evidence of effectiveness. Unfortunately this is often not the case, especially where the media press politicians to respond to each day's "crisis". Often, this leads to a stream of poorly thought-through initiatives based on superficial analyses, although their populist nature has the advantage of attracting favourable newspaper headlines. The state should also take measures to implement its policies as action is needed to enforce legislation. This is shown by experience in areas as diverse as under-age drinking, seat-belt wearing and the use of mobile phones when driving. Equally, it is important to ensure that measures have popular acceptance, often by confronting powerful vested interests that seek to persuade the population to act in ways that endanger their health. In all countries, advertising by junk food manufacturers far exceeds efforts by health promotion agencies. For many years skilful (and highly paid) lobbyists for the tobacco industry were able to persuade people that second-hand smoke was simply an irritation rather than a potentially lethal combination of toxins. In the United Kingdom, debate about the respective roles of the individual and the state has been distorted by frequent disparaging use of the term "nanny state" by those who oppose government intervention in any aspect of life. Failure to resolve this debate means that those charged with implementing policies must first sort out the philosophical confusion (McKee and Raine 2005).

In summary, even most individualistic countries have always shown a degree of acceptance that the state is justified in intervening to improve health. There is now a growing understanding of the importance of doing so in a coherent way that is underpinned by an explicit philosophy; recognizes the challenges that many people face when making healthy choices; is based on evidence of effectiveness; and accompanied by measures that will allow it to work.

At the same time, it should not be assumed that everyone will welcome a health strategy, much less one that incorporates targets. A proposal to develop a health strategy assumes that society as a whole has an interest in the health of the individuals that comprise it. As noted above, even today this view is only partially accepted in many countries where responsibility for obtaining health care is seen largely as a matter for the individual. Thus, what most Europeans would see as a promise of government-funded health care for all is seen as a threat by many American politicians (even if limited to children, as apparent in the failure to pass legislation on the State Children's Health Insurance Program in 2007). Even where there is acceptance of societal responsibility to pay for health care, there is often a view that the system should simply respond to those who seek care rather than actively seeking them out, interfering in the care they receive, or taking action to prevent them needing care in the first place. If someone is unaware that they have a condition that might benefit from treatment, it is for them to educate themselves and to determine what package of care, from the many on offer, best meets their needs. It is assumed that (with the help of an Internet search engine) they can acquire the expertise needed to ascertain the most effective treatment, disregarding the often enticing promises of quacks and charlatans.

A fifth factor contributes to growing societal interest in health and health care – increasing concern about upward pressure on the cost of care. If society pays collectively for health care, it is legitimate to ensure that the care provided is effective, not wasted and, where possible, measures have been taken to avoid the illness arising in the first place. This is the major consideration underlying the Wanless Report (Wanless 2001). This detailed analysis commissioned by HM Treasury in the United Kingdom revealed that the best way to make the cost of future health care sustainable was to act to reduce the likelihood of becoming ill. Of course, this should be self-evident but it is a sad reflection of the disconnect between health care and health promotion in many politicians' minds. The corollary is that if people want to obtain care that has not been proven effective (such as homeopathy) then they can always pay for it themselves.

Taken together, these considerations have led governments in many countries to explore a number of mechanisms that are linked to health policies. They include proactive assessment of health needs; development of guidance on what forms of care are effective, and in what circumstances; and monitoring health outcomes to ensure that what is theoretically possible is being delivered in practice. In some places these developments have been brought together in the form of programmes based on health targets. In such programmes, an organization (whose precise role and configuration will depend on the health system within which it exists) will state what it wants to achieve for the health of a given population and when it expects it to be achieved.

This chapter continues with a summary of the historical development of health targets and then looks briefly at two key issues – who should be responsible and what information do they need?

The emergence of health targets

Health targets draw on the concept of management by objectives which emerged in the 1970s from the literature on new public management. This included closer scrutiny of areas that had been the preserve of professionals through the use of performance measurement, target setting and linkage between resource allocation and measurable outputs. One of its disciples, Peter Drucker (Drucker 1954), identified five key elements of this approach:

1. cascading of organizational goals and objectives
2. specific objectives for each member
3. participative decision-making
4. use of explicit time periods
5. performance evaluation and feedback.

A large body of literature has grown up and provides increasing insights into how these elements can be employed. For example, there has been much discussion about the relative merits of goals that are process or outcome oriented even though, in reality, this is a false dichotomy. While there is little debate about the ultimate importance of achieving changes in outcome, it is also recognized that this may take a long time. For example, an intervention that is extremely effective in preventing young people from starting to smoke now will reduce the subsequent rate of lung cancer, but that change may not be detectable for 30 years. In such a case it is clearly more useful to measure success in terms of reduction in smoking initiation.

Other debates have focused on the extent to which targets should set a general direction of travel or should be detailed road maps, indicating every point along the way. This has been addressed by the separation of aspirational, managerial and technical targets, ranked in terms of the extent to which they prescribe what should be achieved and how (van Herten and Gunning-Schepers 2000).

Similarly, much has been written about the optimal characteristics of targets. At the risk of simplification this literature has been reduced to the SMART mnemonic described in the introduction. In many ways the target-based approach was simply a formalization of processes undertaken in the commercial sector for many decades, symbolized by the sales chart on the chief executive's wall. The introduction of the concept into the health sector is often traced to the publication, in 1981, of WHO's Health for All strategy (WHO 1985). This represented a radical departure from the prevailing approach. It suggested that the progress of nations might be measured not just by their economic progress, using conventional measures such as gross national product, but by the health of their populations. Paradoxically, this represented a return to an earlier time. Before the modern system of national accounts was established in the post Second World War era, the strength of a nation was often assessed in terms of its population, although the focus was on numbers rather than health.

Recognizing the extent of global diversity, each of WHO's regional offices was charged with developing its own set of targets appropriate to the challenges facing its Member States. The most comprehensive approach was taken by the WHO Regional Office for Europe. This initiated a major consultation process that led to the creation of 38 separate targets covering many aspects of health (WHO Regional Office for Europe 1985). The intention was that they should be achieved by 2000, consistent with the stated aspiration that that date would see the achievement of health for all. The targets varied greatly – some were ambitious, aspirational and probably unachievable; others were highly specific and required only a small improvement in existing trends. Some focused on structures and processes, others on outcomes. Inevitably, only some were achieved and often only in some countries. By the mid 1990s, when it was clear that complete success was not forthcoming (and it was unlikely that it ever would have been) (WHO Regional Office for Europe 1998) it was decided to renew the process. Health21, a health strategy for the twenty-first century, retained health targets but reduced their number to reflect the name of the strategy (WHO Regional Office for Europe 1999). It built on some of the lasting legacies of the previous strategy, in particular the substantial strengthening of information systems exemplified by the widely used Health for All database.

Initial development of the Health for All targets involved over 250 experts from across Europe and inevitably impacted on policies within national governments, as did developments elsewhere. For example, the American Government's Healthy People 2000 programme, launched in 1979 (Surgeon General 1979), was renewed in 1990 and incorporated a number of specific health targets. The Health for All process had itself stimulated many governments to develop strategies to improve health, which (as already noted) often produced a new way of thinking about the role of government. A growing number of these strategies included some form of targets (McKee and Berman 2000).

Who is responsible?

Health is everyone's business – this statement has become almost a cliché. It has the advantage of reminding us that we all play a part in improving our own health and that of others. Yet, too easily, it can be used as an excuse to see the leadership to promote health as someone else's responsibility, with that someone else often undefined. These issues lie at the heart of strategies based on health targets. First, how to ensure the widest possible engagement of those working in sectors as diverse as housing, transport, education and fiscal policy;

and in the public, private and nongovernmental sectors? Each must understand that they have a role in the promotion of health but it must be recognized that (while important for society) it is incidental to achieving their main objectives. Second, given that these actors have not come together spontaneously to promote health, who is in charge of creating the mechanisms that will allow them to do so?

Invariably, the answers to these questions will be: it depends (McKee and Fulop 2000). Each country and region has its own system of government. Europe comprises countries that are unitary (e.g. Luxembourg), federal (e.g. Germany), confederal (e.g. Switzerland) and hybrid (e.g. the United Kingdom). Within each there is an enormous diversity of relationships between those potentially involved in a health strategy. Thus, in many countries with a strong tradition of liberal professions, the idea that the state will instruct physicians on how to conduct their practice is likely to be rejected as an unwarranted interference in the doctor-patient relationship, a relationship governed by professional self-regulation. In contrast, in a few countries (most notably the United Kingdom), primary-care physicians are expected to deliver care according to an extremely detailed set of protocols established by the state, with remuneration linked to achievement of the specified standards of care. Tightly specified protocols (prikazes) also characterized the old Soviet health system and persist in many of the ex-Soviet republics, including the Russian Federation. The relationships between actors are also changing. Many countries have privatized major areas that were once core state activities, such as railways, postal deliveries and telecommunications. In such circumstances, very different approaches are needed to build coalitions for health. Command and control must give way to regulation, persuasion and appeals to mutual self-interest.

Who, then, is in charge in practice? The most comprehensive assessment of health targets in Europe was published in 1998 (van de Water and van Herten 1998). It revealed that most countries had formally adopted the concept of health targets, as set out by WHO, and some had recognized the importance of aspiring to reach them. However, very few had gone further to set health targets, put policies or mechanisms in place to achieve them or allow progress towards them to be tracked. Yet, this was not to be decried. In many countries this was the first time that an aspiration to improve population health had been articulated.

In some countries, health policy is the responsibility of regional authorities rather than central government. Contrary to what may be thought, this often enables health to be placed somewhat higher on the political agenda. This may be because chief ministers at regional level are less distracted by foreign affairs, defence etc. Many of the most successful health strategies (in particular those that have employed targets) have been developed at regional level. This book contains several examples such as those from Catalonia or Flanders.

The detailed experiences of regions and countries that have adopted target-based policies are examined in chapters 5 to 11. However, two issues are discussed beforehand. The first is the process of obtaining the information needed to set and monitor targets. The second concerns the establishment of mechanisms to achieve the targets. The process of target setting itself (including the selection of indicators), monitoring and evaluation is examined in detail in Chapter 3.

Information for health targets

In order to set health targets, it is necessary to know the nature of the problem they are to address. This involves collecting and analysing relevant information on the health of the population of interest. Unfortunately, it soon became clear to the pioneers of health targets that often such information is very limited.

The scale of the challenge is apparent from a simple conceptualization of the determinants of health and disease. Europe is unusual in at least having reasonable data on mortality in all countries; most have almost complete coverage of deaths classified by age, sex and cause. European countries also have reasonably accurate data on population sizes, derived from censuses or, more recently, population registers. However, there are some exceptions in countries that have experienced major conflict, for example those in the Caucasus or the former Yugoslavian countries where registration systems broke down in the 1990s. Elsewhere, few countries have valid data on morbidity, beyond notifications of certain infectious diseases. Cancer registries are important sources of data but only a few countries have coverage of the entire population. Worse, some previously well-functioning registries have been damaged by the application of poorly judged data protection laws, as has been the case in Estonia (McKee and Raine 2005). Data on the prevalence of other noncommunicable diseases are largely nonexistent outside a few schemes based on research networks. Most of these provide either nationwide coverage of rare diseases or geographically localized systems covering more common ones.

Data on the immediate risk factors for disease, such as smoking or alcohol consumption, are also fragmentary. Only a few countries conduct annual health surveys although it is self-evident that regular surveys using consistent data definitions, permitting disaggregation by sociodemographic character-istics, are needed if governments are to track progress towards targets and identify those groups at risk. Sampling methods (in particular criteria such as age ranges and inclusion of institutionalized populations), inconsistent questions and inadequate sample sizes limit the scope for analysis and, of particular importance when setting targets, comparison with other countries. Information on the social determinants of health is even more elusive. Very few countries incorporate measures of social class or income; most rely on measures such as educational attainment. In many countries, data protection legislation precludes gathering information on ethnicity, so the specific health needs of ethnic minorities are often unknowable and consequently ignored.

For these reasons, investment in data collection was one of the first actions in some countries exploring the possibility of developing health targets. This is exemplified by the case of England. Unusually, data on social class has been collected since the 1920s but it was apparent that an enhanced data-collection system was needed to track changes in morbidity and risk factors. The Health Survey for England is now conducted annually, using consistent questions but with additional modules or enhanced sampling of particular groups from time to time. It provides a model that could usefully be emulated. Elsewhere (in Sweden, for example) the need to ensure valid data has led to investment in new institutional structures (Swedish National Institute of Public Health 2005). However, data collection is only the first step. It is also necessary to analyse what is already available (Crombie et al. 2003). This is a challenge in many countries given the serious shortage of trained epidemiologists in many parts of Europe.

Implementing health targets

Effective mechanisms are necessary to facilitate the implementation of targets once they have been set. The process becomes even more challenging when strategies require a number of actors from different sectors. Experience shows that implementation tends to be more successful where targets are clearly defined. For instance, in England, targets are core elements of the public service agreements (PSAs) between HM Treasury (Finance Ministry) and spending ministries (such as health) (HM Treasury 1999). In essence, government funding is linked to the achievement of targets. More detailed targets are then developed and monitored within each ministry. One example, discussed later, was the introduction of targets to reduce the number of people spending more than four hours in hospital Accident and Emergency departments, or waiting beyond a specified time for an outpatient appointment or elective surgery. These targets were effective in changing the behaviour of providers, in both intended (so that waiting times fell) and unintended ways (giving rise to a variety of gaming strategies). Targets were also linked to financial incentives in Catalonia (Tresserras et al. 2000). In both cases, public reporting of progress was a further mechanism to encourage a managerial focus on targets.

Given the many determinants of health, involving actions by organizations in many different sectors, effective coordination has emerged as a key issue. The coordination site depends on the structures already in place, in particular the system of governance and the forums within which key actors can meet. This may be easier where responsibility for health lies within local or regional government, as in Scandinavia (Crombie et al. 2003) but, as the example of North Rhine-Westphalia shows (Weihrauch 2000), it is possible to convene relevant actors from many different sectors in other ways. Of course, while stressing the need to involve the many sectors whose actions contribute to health, it is important not to forget about the health-care sector, as often happens (Busse and Wismar 2002).

Whatever model is chosen, it is important to develop a sense of ownership among those who will be called upon to implement health strategies. Unfortunately, as a previous review has noted, this is often not the case: strategies are disseminated in a top-down manner with little effort to ensure involvement of key actors at the grass-roots level (Wismar and Busse 2002).

Some initial conclusions

Health targets are simply a means to an end. They are useful only if they are embedded within a health strategy that sets out a clear view of what is to be achieved. In turn, this requires a shared acceptance that society has a legitimate role in promoting health. In reality, health strategies are simply missing. Often those that do exist are philosophically confused, based on inadequate information and incorporating policies that are devoid of evidence, with no clear idea of where they are going. Health targets are unlikely to help in such circumstances.

The basic health strategy that is being pursued must be identified in order to set targets. This requires information on the existing health of the population concerned, including variations among different subgroups defined in terms of education, income, ethnicity and any other way that will affect the ability to ensure that no one is left behind. Information collection is not a one-off event. Regular monitoring systems are required in order to be able to ascertain whether progress is being made. While the ultimate goal is to improve health outcomes, measures of process will often be more sensitive indicators of pace and the direction being travelled.

The next step is to establish mechanisms to implement targets. There is no simple guide to how this should be done as each model depends on existing systems of governance and linkages between key actors. It may be easier to implement targets in settings where health policy is devolved to regional or local government, where ministers are not distracted by other concerns. However, target-based strategies can work in any system, providing the mechanisms are appropriate.

Finally, it is not enough to set targets, establish mechanisms to design the policies required to hit them and then assume that all will be well. There is a clear need for systems to monitor progress and for appropriate incentives. These should recognize people's ingenuity in finding ways to hit targets by producing the opposite effect from what is intended. Setting and monitoring health targets is a highly skilled occupation, demanding constant vigilance.

The following chapters contain more detailed examination of the information required to establish and monitor progress towards targets, and the governance systems within which they are embedded. Opportunities and pitfalls are identified by reviewing experiences with health targets in a number of European countries. No one has solved all the problems but, by bringing these experiences to a wider audience, it is hoped that it will encourage them to draw on the successes and avoid repeating the failures.

REFERENCES

Busse R, Wismar M (2002). Health target programmes and health care services — any link? A conceptual and comparative study (part 1). *Health Policy,* 59(3):209-221.

Cochrane AL (1972). *Effectiveness and efficiency : random reflections on health services.* London, The Nuffield Provincial Hospitals Trust.

Crombie IK et al. (2003). *Understanding public health policy — learning from international comparisons. A report to NHS Health Scotland.* Glasgow, Public Health Institute of Scotland.

Diethelm PA, Rielle JC, McKee M (2005). The whole truth and nothing but the truth? The research that Philip Morris did not want you to see. *Lancet,* 366(9479):86-92.

Drucker PF (1954). *Practice of management.* New York, Harper.

Ezzati M et al., eds. (2004). *Comparative quantification of health risks, global and regional burden of disease attributable to selected major risk factors.* Geneva, World Health Organization.

HM Treasury (1999). *Public services for the future: modernization, reform, accountability.* London, The Stationery Office.

Houston DJ, Richardson LE Jr. (2007). Motorcycle safety and the repeal of universal helmet laws. *American Journal of Public Health,* 97(11): 2063-2069.

Marinker M (2002). *Health targets in Europe: policy, progress and promise.* London, BMJ Books.

McKee M, Berman PC (2000). Health targets in Europe: learning from experience. *European Journal of Public Health,* 10(Suppl. 4):1.

McKee M, Colagiuri R (2007). What are governments for? *Medical Journal of Australia,* 187(11-12):654-655.

McKee M, Fulop N (2000). On target for health? Health targets may be valuable, but context is all important. *BMJ,* 320(7231):327-328.

McKee M, Raine R (2005). Choosing health? First choose your philosophy. *Lancet,* 365(9457):369-371.

Mill JS (2003). *On liberty.* New Haven and London, Yale University Press.

Nolte E, McKee CM (2008). Measuring the health of nations: updating an earlier analysis. *Health Affairs,* 27(1):58-71.

Nolte E, McKee M (2004). *Does healthcare save lives? Avoidable mortality revisited.* London, The Nuffield Trust.

Suhrcke M et al. (2006). Investment in health could be good for Europe's economies. *BMJ,* 333(7576):1017-1019.

Surgeon General (1979). *Healthy people. The Surgeon General's Report on Health Promotion and Disease Prevention.* Washington DC, US Department of Health Education and Welfare.

Swedish National Institute of Public Health (2005). *The 2005 Public Health Policy Report.* Stockholm, Swedish National Institute of Public Health.

Tresserras R et al. (2000). Health targets and priorities in Catalonia, Spain. *European Journal of Public Health,* 10(Suppl. 4):51-56.

van de Water HPA, van Herten LM (1998). *Health policies on target? Review of health target and priority setting in 18 European countries.* Leiden, TNO.

van Herten LM, Gunning-Schepers LJ (2000). Targets as a tool in health policy. Part I: lessons learned. *Health Policy,* 53(1):1-11.

Wanless D (2001). *Securing our future health: taking a long-term view; interim report.* London, HM Treasury, Public Enquiry Unit

Weihrauch B (2000). Health targets as a means of a rational health policy in North Rhine-Westphalia. *European Journal of Public Health,* 10(Suppl. 4):34-37.

Wismar M, Busse R (2002). Outcome-related health targets — political strategies for better health outcomes: a conceptual and comparative study (part 2). *Health Policy,* 59(3):223-241.

WHO Regional Office for Europe (1999). *Health21: the Health for All policy framework for the WHO European Region.* Copenhagen, WHO Regional Office for Europe.

WHO Regional Office for Europe (1998). *Health in Europe 1997. Report on the third evaluation of progress towards Health for All in the European Region of WHO (1996-1997).* Copenhagen, WHO Regional Office for Europe.

WHO Regional Office for Europe (1985). *Targets for Health for All. Targets in support of the European regional strategy for health for all.* Copenhagen, WHO Regional Office for Europe.

Chapter 3

On Target? Monitoring and Evaluation

Martin McKee

Introduction

This chapter examines the main technical issues involved in target setting. It begins from three simple, but crucial, premises. First, those charged with hitting a target can reasonably be expected to do so within the means at their disposal and the timescale given. Second, a target should be sufficiently challenging to stimulate new and better ways of doing things rather than simply waiting for nature to take its course. Third, if the ultimate goal of a health system is to promote the health of the population served, then a target should at least be on an established pathway towards better health (even if not itself involving an improvement in health).

These premises have important implications for those setting targets. They must understand the pathways from health to disease and back again. This includes the etiology of the diseases with which they are concerned; the way in which risk factors interact and the timescales over which they operate; the policies and interventions effective in tackling disease and the timescales over which they operate. Unfortunately, as the case studies illustrate (chapters 5-11), this knowledge may not always be available or, if it is, is not always used.

What is the ultimate goal?

Those setting targets for improved health face a major problem – the very limited range of outcomes available to them. Frequently, they have only the information on death rates generated by vital registration systems. Consequently, health targets often take the form: to reduce the death rate from disease X. While a reduction in deaths from a particular disease is clearly a desirable goal, it suffers from two main limitations.

First, it fails to capture the non-fatal consequences of disease. A set of targets focused on mortality reduction may give less than optimal attention to diseases where the outcome is often non-fatal. For example, it would tend to favour cancer over mental health. It may focus disproportionate attention on some groups within a population. For example, mortality in the Russian Federation is much higher among men so any policies arising from a target to reduce overall mortality would inevitably focus on their needs. However, Russian women who survive into older age have very high levels of ill health – there is a gap of over 12 years in life expectancy at birth between the sexes but only a 4-year gap in healthy life expectancy (Andreev et al. 2003). The policies pursued will depend on the target that is set.

Second, as discussed in more detail later, many policies that will reduce mortality often do so far in the future. For example, a policy that reduces smoking will benefit some people almost at once (e.g. those with ischaemic heart disease because of the reduction in carbon monoxide in their blood). However, benefits from a lower risk of lung and other cancers will only become apparent after a decade or more. Yet, given the well-established causal link between smoking and lung cancer (Doll and Hill 1964), it is entirely reasonable to set a target to reduce smoking in the firm knowledge that it will ultimately lead to better health outcomes.

Previous reviews of the process of health target programmes have highlighted the frequent necessity to establish new systems of data collection in order to be able to set and monitor targets (Fulop et al. 2000). One example is the Health Survey for England, an annual health and lifestyle survey developed to support the Health of the Nation strategy. Unfortunately, many European countries lag far behind the United States of America where the creation of a range of ongoing surveys makes it possible to track changes in health-related behaviours (Behavioral Risk Factor Surveillance System – BRFSS) or risk factors (National Health and Nutrition Examination Survey – NHANES) at the level of individual states. Where such sources of information are lacking a health target programme is forced to focus on what is measured.

This can easily undermine the use of targets, as illustrated by the mental-health element of the English Health of the Nation strategy and its successor, Our Healthier Nation (Fulop et al. 2000). The former used the reduction of the suicide rate in a defined population as a target for mental-health services. Those responsible for achieving the target reasonably pointed out that, first, this focus on what was easily measured disregarded the vast majority of their work as they did much more than prevent suicide. Second, many of the determinants of suicide lay far outside their control, such as access to the means of committing suicide. For example, numbers declined following the change from coal gas (containing carbon monoxide) to natural gas (consisting of methane) (Kreitman 1976) or the introduction of catalytic converters in cars that also reduced access to carbon monoxide (Kelly and Bunting 1998). Similarly, it was well-known that suicide rates were influenced by the performance of the national economy (Wasserman 1984). Yet although it was apparent that this target had little credibility among those charged with achieving it, it was retained in the later strategy because there was no obvious alternative.

What counts cannot necessarily be counted

Those involved in promoting health or delivering health care do so in a challenging environment. The goals are often complex and potentially competing, unlike private industry where the goal is simply to maximize returns to shareholders. This can be illustrated by consideration of how the performance of a hospital can be measured. A simplistic approach might be to measure the number of patients treated. This is straightforward where patients have a condition that can be cured by a single specialist team during a single attendance or admission. Yet such cases are a minority and many patients require long-term interactions with a complex combination of different specialists, especially as populations age (Clarke and McKee 1992). This is exemplified by an increasingly common disease – diabetes. This may affect many body systems. A patient with severe complications may require an ophthalmologist to treat diabetic eye disease; a vascular surgeon to treat arterial disease in the legs; a cardiologist to treat heart disease; as well as an endocrinologist and a dietitian to help manage the diabetes. Furthermore, hospitals do much more than treat patients (McKee and Healy 2002). All but the smallest facilities are likely to provide training for the next generation of health professionals. They may also be the sites of important health-related research and, by contributing to the local economy, may sustain a community that would otherwise decline.

It is essential to bear in mind these multiple goals when setting targets – the pursuit of one should not adversely affect the others. A focus on the easily measurable (such as numbers of surgical procedures) should not divert attention from others in equal need but whose care may be less easy to measure. Mental health is the classic example of this.

Defining disease

As noted above, health targets frequently involve making a statement about a particular disease, typically in relation to reducing mortality from it. Benjamin

Franklin famously said: "In this world nothing can be said to be certain, except death and taxes"(Franklin and Sparks 1844).

The international standard for death certification provides for listing of the disease or condition that leads directly to death, as well as other conditions giving rise to that cause and other conditions contributing to death but not related to the condition causing it. But while the fact of death is usually quite unambiguous, the cause may not be. The International Classification of Diseases (ICD) incorporates explicit rules for determining the underlying cause of death. This is used in most basic tabulations and is defined as the disease or injury which initiated the train of morbid events leading directly to death; or the circumstances of the accident or violence which produced the fatal injury (World Health Organization 1993).

In other words, the underlying cause of death is the condition, event or circumstances in the absence of which the individual would not have died. For example, a person with cancer dies but the immediate cause of death was heart failure as a consequence of carcinomatosis. The original neoplasm site was in the stomach but heart failure was the final event in the sequence that began with cancer of the stomach. The stomach cancer is identified as the underlying cause of death.

In practice, especially at older ages, death may be the final event in a process involving multiple diseases. This poses a major challenge to those seeking to determine what was actually responsible for the terminal event. Think, for example, of an elderly individual with dementia, heart failure, chronic obstructive pulmonary disease and kidney failure. While pneumonia may be the ultimate cause of death it may be quite difficult to decide which of the other conditions was the underlying cause, and therefore to which category the death should be allocated.

The situation is complicated further when targets span several of the periodic revisions of the ICD. These are necessary to take account of newly emerging diseases, such as AIDS, or changes in the understanding of disease processes, such as the differentiation of the various forms of diabetes. However, revisions can complicate the monitoring of health targets, especially where there are changes in the rules for allocating the underlying cause of death. For example, consider a death certificate that lists the immediate cause of death as pneumonia and Parkinson's disease as contributing to death, but not directly related to the condition causing it. Using the rules set out in the ninth revision this would be recorded as a death from pneumonia; the tenth revision would record it as a death from Parkinson's (Office of National Statistics 2002).

In all but a few cases (such as a bone fracture) there is a progression from health to disease. This leads to potential uncertainty about the threshold above which disease is deemed to be present. This can change over time, particularly when new technology makes it possible to detect changes that would previously have been missed. For example, following the introduction of an assay for troponin, a substance released into the blood following a myocardial infarction, it soon became clear that it was a much more sensitive indicator of infarction than conventional cardiac enzymes. This resulted in the diagnosis of many cases that would previously have been excluded. In one study the use of troponin assays increased the number of patients with myocardial infarctions by 58%. Importantly, the additional cases tended to have worse prognoses so a hospital that introduced this assay would compromise its ability to achieve a target to reduce mortality following myocardial infarction (Pell et al. 2003).

The issue of diagnostic thresholds also arises in another situation. A target for health facilities may seek to take account of differences in the case-mix of patients treated. Algorithms can be developed to adjust for the severity of each patient's illness, based on records of the comorbid conditions and their complications (Iezzoni 1997). However, as with the main diagnosis, there is often considerable scope for debate about the threshold for recording these other conditions. This becomes particularly problematic where there is external pressure to achieve a target. The clinicians involved have a powerful incentive to record the presence of a condition even if there is some doubt about whether the threshold has been reached. This has been seen, for example, in settings where authorities have required facilities to publish death rates following particular procedures – the frequency of recording comorbidities has often risen markedly, despite any objective evidence that the patients have become sicker (Green and Wintfeld 1995).

When can we expect to see change?

Perhaps inevitably, politicians frequently wish to see the benefits of their policies as soon as possible. This may not be possible for health matters as it is dependent on the natural history of the disease process involved. In some cases the interval between exposure to a risk factor and a health outcome is almost instantaneous. Thus, individuals who go out, drink until they become inebriated and then attempt to drive home can reasonably expect to be killed. In contrast, someone who takes up smoking as a teenager is likely to have at least as high a risk of dying as a consequence of their decision (50% of smokers die as a result of their smoking; 50% of these will die before retirement age) yet the interval between taking up smoking and premature death may be several decades.

The Soviet Union provides two good examples. Concerned about the impact of widespread drunkenness on absenteeism from work, and hence on Soviet economic performance, Mikhail Gorbachev introduced a wide-ranging and initially highly effective anti-alcohol campaign in 1985 (White 1995). The impact on mortality was dramatic, with deaths falling almost at once (Leon et al. 1997). In contrast, Stalin made strenuous efforts to ensure that cigarettes were freely available to the Red Army during the Second World War, even at the expense of food and ammunition. Thus, the prevalence of smoking was very high among the generation of men who reached late adolescence at this time. After the war ended, the Soviet regime concentrated on rebuilding the country's industrial infrastructure and consumer goods of all sorts (including cigarettes) were much less easily available. After Stalin's death, Krushchev sought to buttress his position by prioritizing consumer goods and cigarettes again became widely available. The consequences of these changes only became fully apparent decades later. The sustained decline in lung cancer mortality in the Russian Federation seen during the 1990s was a consequence of lower smoking rates among those reaching adolescence between 1945 and 1953 (Shkolnikov et al. 1999).

The rapid health effects of changes in alcohol consumption are apparent from other natural experiments, such as the rationing of alcohol in France during the Nazi occupation (Ledermann 1964). A reduction in mortality from cirrhosis was apparent almost at once (Figure 3-1). Conversely, the increase in cigarette consumption in the United Kingdom preceded the rise in lung cancer mortality by about three decades (Figure 3-2).

Figure 3-1 *Wine rationing: effect on mortality from liver cirrhosis in Paris*

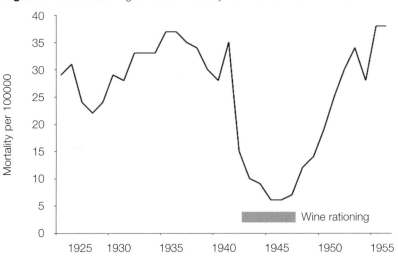

Source: Ledermann, 1964

Figure 3-2 *Smoking and lung cancer in British men*

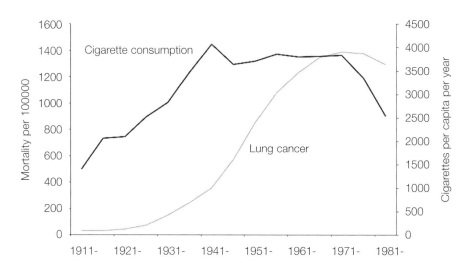

Note: data on men aged 45+

Source: data from Forey et al. 2002

However, these two examples also illustrate an important aspect of the relationship between many exposures and disease – it is often asymmetrical. It may take a population many years of exposure to a risk factor for death rates from a disease to climb whereas withdrawal of that risk factor may produce a rapid reduction in mortality. This has been explained by an analogy to a conveyor belt, in which the period of exposure is likened to the lengthy ascent of the conveyor belt, with death occurring when one falls over the end (Leon DA, personal communication). However, stopping the movement of the belt will allow those on it to avoid dropping off the end.

Time also comes into play for some clinical interventions that may be the subject of health targets. The effectiveness of cancer treatment is usually measured as the percentage of patients surviving five years. Obviously, this means that outcomes of treatment provided now can be available after at least five years. In practice, delays in analysing and publishing data mean that the interval may be even longer.

Who is being targeted?

Populations are increasingly mobile. The advent of low-cost air travel has enabled unprecedented numbers of people to move between countries, in some cases spending part of their week working in one and moving to another for the weekend. Within Europe, the lowering of borders following the 2004 enlargement of the EU has stimulated a large scale process of migration from some of the new Member States to their western European neighbours (McKee et al. 2004).

Some places have long been characterized by large-scale migration. The East End of London has seen successive waves of migrants settle before moving on, such as European Jews in the 1930s and Bangladeshis in the 1980s. Long-term health targets must take account of the population dynamics in areas such as these, as 20% or more of the population may move every year. Thus, an intervention aimed at the population of an area today may bring benefits to those individuals when they are living somewhere entirely different many years in the future, for example a target to reduce death rates from cancer.

The impact of unrecorded migration is a related issue. In many countries distrust of authorities coupled with more mobile populations means that censuses are becoming less accurate measures of population size and characteristics. For example, a London local government authority successfully mounted a legal challenge against the Office for National Statistics on the grounds that the 2001 census had undercounted its resident population, with important financial consequences (Statistics Commission 2003). However, the key issue for those involved in monitoring targets is that while deaths will continue to be recorded, unmeasured changes in the population denominator will render rates potentially meaningless.

Moving beyond the average

Applied to populations, health-related policies may achieve their targets by improving the health of only a subset of the population. Improvements in the average can mask either no change or even worse health in some groups. Thus, there is extensive evidence that many policies designed to change behaviour are most effective among those whose needs are least (Mackenbach et al. 2003). The most disadvantaged may face various constraints that prevent them from taking advantage of the opportunities available. In some cases they may be unable to afford to change their behaviour. For example, those on limited incomes may be aware of the benefits of eating more fresh fruit and vegetables but unable to afford them. Also, nutritious food may not be readily accessible as retail outlets seek to maximize their profits by concentrating their resources on wealthy areas (Morland et al. 2002). In other cases, for example where there is a multi-ethnic population, messages may not be communicated because they are not tailored to linguistic or cultural diversity (Kumanyika and Grier 2006).

As a consequence, in many countries health policies have served to widen health inequalities even while producing overall improvements. The United Kingdom had a 1.2-fold difference in the age-standardized mortality ratio between the poorest and the wealthiest social class between 1930 and 1932; by 1991 to 1993 the gap had widened to 2.9-fold. This occurred over a period in which overall mortality was declining markedly (Acheson 1998).

What do targets mean?

There is an inevitable tension between breadth of coverage of health and health care (implying the use of large numbers of targets) and simplicity (implying a much smaller number). Some authorities have sought to address this by producing composite targets, several examples of which can be found in the 1998 proposals for targets in the English NHS. One of the targets selected to assess preventive services was a combination of the percentage of the population vaccinated and the percentage of all orchidopexies below age 5 (an indicator of the effectiveness of detecting undescended testes at an early stage) (McKee and Sheldon 1998). It is entirely conceivable that a district might score high on one of these measures but low on the other, and a real problem might be missed.

Dealing with uncertainty

In some cases an outcome is desirable but, at the level of analysis involved, the frequency of events is so low that it becomes impossible to disentangle an effect of an intervention from background noise. The frequency of virtually any event is associated with a degree of random variation, exemplified by the school experiment of tossing a coin to determine the distribution of heads and tails. Well-established statistical tests can establish the probability that a difference in the frequency of events in different periods or in different places is unlikely to be due to chance. The word "unlikely" is important. Conventionally, statistical tests involving a limited number of comparisons take it to mean that there is less than a one in twenty probability that the difference was due to chance. Clearly, even in such circumstances, it is impossible to exclude the play of chance completely. This becomes increasingly important as the event frequency becomes smaller. Thus, a target that envisages a reduction in the frequency of an event that is already rare should be treated with great caution.

A contemporary example is the English Department of Health's use of a target to reduce the number of cases of infection with methicillin-resistant

Staphylococcus aureus (MRSA), a form of hospital-acquired infection that is very difficult to eradicate (Health Protection Agency 2006). This developed great political importance as opposition politicians used figures on the frequency of infection to attack the government on their record on hospital cleanliness. Hospital chief executives could expect serious repercussions if the number of infections had increased from the previous year. Yet it was accepted that it would be difficult for a hospital to eliminate cases entirely. Despite stringent precautions, there was the potential for infections to be brought in on transferred patients and perhaps detected only in the receiving hospital. Furthermore, in many hospitals the number of infections was already in single figures. A hospital could be castigated for a 100% increase in cases (e.g. from two to four), all of which might have been outside their control.

An analogous problem occurs where there is a desire to focus on outcomes, even though the relationship between the intervention and the outcome means that there will be only a small change in outcome. This was illustrated in a paper that looked at a variety of potential measures of performance in relation to the management of ischaemic heart disease at the level of individual hospitals (Mant and Hicks 1995). It was known that an increase in the proportion of patients with heart attacks who received thrombolytic (clot-busting) drugs would reduce mortality among affected patients. When measured by outcome targets (in this case, mortality following a heart attack) it was calculated that it would require 73 years to obtain enough data from a typical hospital to be reasonably certain that there had been a clinically significant reduction in mortality. Conversely, four months of data on process measures (in this case the percentage of patients receiving treatment) would reveal whether the desired change in treatment had been accomplished.

Of course, it is necessary to be sure that the process measure used can be expected to lead to an improved outcome. This is not always the case. For example, in 1998 one of the proposed targets for the English NHS was the rate of district-nurse contacts with people over 75. This measure was essentially meaningless in the absence of information about either the extent of underlying need or the effectiveness of what was done during those contacts (McKee and Sheldon 1998).

Playing games

The philosophy underlying the use of health targets is that they should stimulate those charged with achieving them to act in a way that, ultimately, improves health. Yet there is often much scope for individuals and organizations to engage in opportunistic behaviour, especially where targets are poorly designed or seen as being imposed from outside (Smith 1995). This is often referred to as Goodhart's Law, named after the chief adviser to the Bank of England who proposed it. This states that once a social or economic indicator is made a target for the purpose of conducting social or economic policy, it loses the information content that qualifies it to play such a role (Goodhart 1975). Its use will create powerful incentives for those involved either to distort the data or to engage in other forms of gaming that render it useless.

As Smith notes elsewhere in this book, much of the early evidence on this topic comes from the Soviet Union, where managers were exhorted to achieve the targets set out in successive five-year plans. Given the penalties for failure it is not surprising that they were usually successful, often because they behaved in ways that were not anticipated by those setting the targets (Nove 1980). There is an apocryphal Russian saying: "ten people in the Kremlin were engaged in setting the targets while thousands of people throughout the country worked to circumvent them". One approach was to put enormous effort into achieving the target while disregarding all else. This gave rise to the term Stakhanovite, after the Ukrainian miner Stakhanov, who was held up as an example because of his ability to hew 227 tonnes of coal in a single shift (Anon 1935). It was not mentioned that he was supported by dozens of others preparing the coalface for him and clearing away the rocks that he cut. Another approach was simply to make up the figures, an activity that gained prominence when it was revealed that officials (including the son-in-law of party secretary Leonid Brezhnev) had been falsifying data on cotton production in Uzbekistan (Kinzer 1997).

Today, the prominence of quantitative targets in the English NHS, coupled with the sanctions against managers who fail to meet them (admittedly less severe than in the Soviet Union), have given rise to numerous examples of similar behaviour (Box 3-1).

However, such responses are not confined to the health sector in the United Kingdom. There are numerous examples throughout the public sector, reflecting ministers' obsession with being able to demonstrate value for money. Thus, in 2007, the Police Federation of England and Wales complained about the prevailing target culture that was pressurizing them to make large numbers of "ludicrous" arrests for trivial actions as these were much easier to clear up than more serious and complex crimes. Examples cited included a child arrested after removing a slice of cucumber from a sandwich and throwing it at another youngster; a woman arrested for criminal damage on her wedding day when she damaged a car park barrier after her foot slipped on her vehicle accelerator pedal; and two children arrested for being in possession of a plastic toy pistol (BBC 2007).

Box 3-1 *Dysfunctional responses to targets in England*

- A conflict arose between ambulance providers, whose target was to reach patients within eight minutes (requiring large numbers of ambulances to be available), and emergency departments, whose target was to transfer or discharge patients within four hours. As the emergency departments did not want to accept patients from ambulances until they were ready for them the ambulances were used as "target-free" waiting areas. The ambulance providers solved this by purchasing tents to erect in hospital car parks.
- A target to treat all patients on a waiting list for non-urgent surgery was achieved by keeping patients on the untargeted waiting list for the initial outpatient appointment (required in order to join the targeted waiting list) as long as possible.
- A target to ensure that all patients obtained an appointment with a general practitioner within 48 hours was achieved by preventing patients from making appointments more than 48 hours in advance. This meant that they had to spend lengthy periods on the telephone on the morning of the day before they wanted an appointment.
- Patients waiting for non-urgent surgery can legitimately be removed from the waiting list if they are offered an operation but do not take it up. Several hospitals called large number of patients in mid summer or just before Christmas, in the expectation that many would be unable to come into hospital.
- Primary care trusts are judged on their achievement of a target to get smokers to quit for at least four weeks. One trust achieved this by paying smokers to do so.
- A hospital seeking foundation trust status (giving it greater independence) sent an e-mail to staff encouraging them to reduce the number of blood cultures undertaken. The context led staff to believe that this was to reduce the reported number of cases of antibiotic-resistant infection as failure to hit the target to reduce such infections would compromise their application.

Source: BBC 2008; Wismar et al. 2006

Returning to the differences in the impact on different groups in the population, it is important to recognize that a target can create incentives to exclude individuals from interventions from which they would benefit. This situation arises where those individuals can be identified as having a worse prognosis and providers are being judged on their outcomes. Thus, the publication of the mortality rates associated with New York's cardiac surgeons was followed by an increase in ethnic disparities in the utilization of surgery; surgeons were aware that African American patients had worse outcomes (Werner et al. 2005).

Clearly, there is tremendous scope for opportunistic behaviour in an area such as health where there is so much uncertainty about whether an individual has a specific disease or what was the cause of death. This could be by simple fraud in recording data or, more insidiously, the introduction of systematic bias while remaining within the limits of diagnostic uncertainty.

What is to be done?

It is apparent from this brief review that the process of developing and monitoring health targets involves a number of technical considerations. It is widely accepted that targets should be SMART. In reality these criteria are often not met, as illustrated in a humorous commentary on government targets published in a British newspaper (Box 3-2).

On the basis of the preceding analysis it is possible to set out an agenda for developing targets that are meaningful and can be evaluated. However, this involves some detailed thinking as well as an appropriate epidemiological and demographic infrastructure that is lacking in too many countries. The targets

Box 3-2 *Glossary of the baffling terms used by Treasury target-setters*

Slippage: a target that has not been met, but might yet be.

Rolled forward: not the Lotto jackpot, but a way of keeping a target going past its sell-by date, rather than admitting it has been missed.

Not met: as near as ministers come to saying "failed" or "broken"; this passes for strong language.

Baseline not verified: baffling term; basically means a target the terms of which are so unclear that it cannot be measured.

Not yet assessed: crops up frequently, a way of keeping a difficult target going indefinitely.

Ongoing: a bit like "rolled forward", only not so specific. Rolled forward carries a slight admission of failure; ongoing is target speak for "we never said this would ever be finished".

On course: "stop asking so many awkward questions, we'll let you know when we're ready".

Measure changed: admission that the original target has been completely revised.

Cannot assess: the Treasury's admission that a target is too baffling to make sense of.

Non-smart: a target that was never meant to be assessed, has no set timetable and no set definition.

Source: Kite 2002

suggested by this process must be tested to see whether the measures involved can be quantified unambiguously; there is sufficient information to determine their baseline; the proposed interventions can reasonably be expected to lead to a change that can be detected with confidence; and the timescale over which change might reasonably be achieved is consistent with the proposed monitoring system. Clearly this requires much more than a few people sitting around a table thinking of what might be interesting to include. There is a need for a devil's advocate – to anticipate how those tasked with achieving a target might engage in opportunistic behaviour to appear to comply while not necessarily increasing human welfare.

It is apparent that nearly all European countries have far too few data on health, health-related behaviour and the use of health services. There is an urgent need to establish ongoing surveys on a scale sufficient to allow the disaggregation necessary to track progress towards targets among different groups within the population. Given the increasing ethnic diversity within Europe, this may require over-sampling of particular groups in some countries. There are some well-established models that can be drawn on. However, given the widely accepted need to incorporate targets for health into EU policies, there is a powerful argument for collaborative working to develop comparable instruments across Europe.

It is essential that targets are based on a clear understanding of the nature of disease and how health care and broader health policies contribute to its reduction. Unfortunately, despite the sterling efforts of many researchers (in particular those participating in the Cochrane Collaboration, who have synthesized the available evidence in many fields) sustained underinvestment in evaluation means that often there is inadequate understanding of what works and in what circumstances. There is an even greater lack of evidence on the cost-effectiveness of many policies.

Health targets should be challenging but achievable. This requires those setting them to have some idea of what would happen to disease trends if nothing was done. Prediction is fraught with problems (McKee 2006). A detailed consideration is beyond the scope of this chapter but it should be noted that there are well-validated methods of forecasting (with an acceptable degree of uncertainty) future trends in many diseases, especially those with long lag periods between exposure and outcome. Often, a starting point is to undertake an age-period-cohort analysis on the basis that changing rates of disease are typically influenced by a combination of the age distribution of the population; events occurring at a particular period; and when people were born and reached different stages in their life. The results of such an analysis can be combined with demographic forecasts of the future composition of the population and with some of the increasingly sophisticated models of the effect of changing risk factors (Naidoo et al. 1997).

Those who set health targets should also understand that medicine is not an exact science. Too often, techniques taken from industrial production are applied unthinkingly to the delivery of health care. Yet many patients will have an almost unique combination of medical conditions, social needs and legitimate expectations about how they will be treated. This is entirely different from producing tins of beans. Despite sustained and expensive attempts to find ways of accounting for the diversity of patients, there is still far to go. Often, case-mix adjustment methods are applied within systems that create powerful incentives for opportunistic behaviour. Also, uncertainty arises when targets involve small numbers of events.

Finally, there is a need to understand that an overall improvement does not necessarily mean that everyone has benefited. By design, health interventions often favour one group over another. There is a need to ensure that systems for monitoring and evaluation identify those at risk of being left behind.

Conclusion

This chapter has described many examples of problems with health targets. It could be read as a counsel of despair, suggesting that it is futile to attempt to develop appropriate targets. Yet this would be quite wrong. Given that only certain aspects of health and health care are easily measurable, quantitative targets (on which this chapter has focused) can be only one part of an overall health strategy. Targets can be meaningful only if such a strategy exists, based on explicit goals.

This book contains many examples of targets that are SMART and have contributed to processes that have led to better health. A clear prerequisite is the involvement of those with appropriate understanding of health and disease and the range of potential interventions and their effectiveness; and the epidemiological, demographic and modelling skills to apply this knowledge. Unfortunately, these skills are in short supply in many parts of Europe; where they do exist they are often undervalued and underused. However, as the examples in this chapter show, perhaps the greatest obstacle to the development of meaningful targets is the political imperative to produce eye-catching populist targets that are incompatible with basic epidemiological and demographic principles. This is exemplified by the situation in England – not only in the health sector, as described here, but across government. Health targets involve technical and political input. One cannot substitute for the other.

Acknowledgement: Several of the themes addressed in this chapter have been refined in constructive conversations with Professor David Leon, London School of Hygiene and Tropical Medicine

REFERENCES

Acheson D (1998). *Independent Inquiry into Inequalities in Health Report.* London, The Stationery Office.

Andreev EM, McKee M, Shkolnikov VM (2003). Health expectancy in the Russian Federation: a new perspective on the health divide in Europe. *Bulletin of the World Health Organization,* 81(11):778-787.

Anon (1935). Heroes of labour. *Time Magazine:*26-27.

BBC (2008). Trust denies massaging MRSA data. BBC News Online (available at: http://news.bbc.co.uk/1/hi/health/7227818.stm, accessed 5 February 2008.

Clarke A, McKee M (1992). The consultant episode: an unhelpful measure. *BMJ,* 305(6865):1307-1308.

Doll R, Hill AB (1964). Mortality in relation to smoking: ten years' observations of British doctors. *BMJ,* 5395:1399-1410.

Forey B et al. (2002). *International smoking statistics: a collection of historical data from 30 economically developed countries. 2nd edition.* London, Oxford University Press.

Franklin B, Sparks J (1844). *The works of Benjamin Franklin; containing several political and historical tracts not included in any former edition.* Boston, Tappan & Whittemore.

Fulop N et al. (2000). Lessons for health strategies in Europe: the evaluation of a national health strategy in England. *European Journal of Public Health,* 10:11-17.

Goodhart CAE (1975). Monetary relationships: a view from Threadneedle Street. In: *Papers in monetary economics, Volume I.* Canberra, Reserve Bank of Australia.

Green J, Wintfeld N (1995). Report cards on cardiac surgeons. Assessing New York State's approach. *The New England Journal of Medicine,* 332(18):1229-1232.

Health Protection Agency (2006). *MRSA surveillance system: results 2006.* Communicable Disease Surveillance Centre, Department of Health

Iezzoni I (1997). The risks of risk adjustment. *Jama,* 278(19):1600-1607.

Kelly S, Bunting J (1998). Trends in suicide in England and Wales, 1982-96. *Population Trends,* (92):29-41.

Kinzer S (1997). Free of Russians, but imprisoned in cotton. *Gazli Journal.* November 20th

Kite M (2002). Labour misses 75% of performance targets. *The Times:*2.

Kreitman N (1976). The coal gas story. United Kingdom suicide rates, 1960-71. *British Journal of Preventive and Social Medicine,* 30(2):86-93.

Kumanyika S, Grier S (2006). Targeting interventions for ethnic minority and low-income populations. *Future Child,* 16(1):187-207.

Ledermann S (1964). *Alcool, alcoolisme, alcoolisation Vol. II. Mortalité, morbidité, accidents du travail.* Paris, Presses Universitaires de France.

Leon DA et al. (1997). Huge variation in Russian mortality rates 1984-94: artefact, alcohol, or what? *Lancet,* 350(9075):383-388.

Mackenbach JP et al. (2003). Widening socioeconomic inequalities in mortality in six western European countries. *International Journal of Epidemiology,* 32(5):830-837.

Mant J, Hicks N (1995). Detecting differences in quality of care: the sensitivity of measures of process and outcome in treating acute myocardial infarction. *BMJ,* 311(7008):793-796.

McKee M (2006). The future. In: Marinker M, ed. *Constructive conversations about health: policy and values.* Oxford, Radcliffe Medical Press:215-229.

McKee M, Healy J (2002). *Hospitals in a changing Europe.* Buckingham, Open University Press.

McKee M, MacLehose L, Nolte E (2004). *Health policy and European Union enlargement.* Buckingham, Open University Press.

McKee M, Sheldon T (1998). Measuring performance in the NHS. *BMJ,* 316(7128):322.

Morland K et al. (2002). Neighborhood characteristics associated with the location of food stores and food service places. *American Journal of Preventive Medicine,* 22(1):23-29.

Naidoo B et al. (1997). Modelling the effects of increased physical activity on coronary heart disease in England and Wales. *J Epidemiol Community Health,* 51(2):144-150.

Nove A (1980). *The Soviet economic system, 2nd edition.* London, Allen and Unwin.

Office for National Statistics (2002). *Examples of death certificates and underlying cause of death in ICD-9 and ICD-10.* London, Office for National Statistics.

Pell JP et al. (2003). Impact of changing diagnostic criteria on incidence, management, and outcome of acute myocardial infarction: retrospective cohort study. *BMJ,* 326(7381):134-135.

Shkolnikov V et al. (1999). Why is the death rate from lung cancer falling in the Russian Federation? *European Journal of Epidemiology,* 15(3):203-206.

Smith P (1995). On the unintended consequences of publishing performance data in the public sector. *International Journal of Public Administration,* 18(2/3):277-310.

Statistics Commission (2003). *The 2001 Census in Westminster: Interim Report.* London, Statistics Commission.

Wasserman IM (1984). The influence of economic business cycles on United States suicide rates. *Suicide Life Threat Behav,* 14(3):143-156.

Werner RM, Asch DA, Polsky D (2005). Racial profiling: the unintended consequences of coronary artery bypass graft report cards. *Circulation,* 111(10):1257-1263.

White S (1995). *Russia goes dry.* Cambridge, Cambridge University Press.

Wismar M et al. (2006). Health targets and (good) governance. *EuroObserver,* 8(Spring):1-8.

World Health Organization (1993). *ICD-10: International statistical classification of diseases and related health problems. Vol. 2. Instruction manual.* Geneva, World Health Organization.

Chapter 4
Improving the Effectiveness of Health Targets

Kelly Ernst, Matthias Wismar, Reinhard Busse, Martin McKee

Introduction

This chapter looks at the ways in which the effectiveness of health targets can be evaluated. Of course, the primary question is whether targets have been achieved (assuming that they are appropriate in the first place). A secondary question is whether the process of developing targets has facilitated the creation of an environment that is more conducive to promoting health, for example by focusing attention on the need for a health strategy; enabling disparate groups to come together for a common purpose; or demonstrating the need to put in place an infrastructure for health intelligence.

At the outset, it is apparent that health targets face major challenges in many situations. Those charged with their development are rarely given the managerial or financial resources to implement the policies necessary to attain them. Instead, they must rely solely upon moral pressure, encouragement and inspiration. There are also situations where targets are accompanied by systems of accountability, with sanctions for failure but insufficient financial resources to bring about change. In England, this phenomenon has been described as "centralizing power but decentralizing blame". Yet, as illustrated in the case studies, some health targets have been used effectively to bring about change. Even where it is too early to identify specific changes in the health of the population, proxy indicators indicate that health gains are plausible in the future.

The second part of the chapter draws on the case studies in this book to examine the different approaches that have been used to achieve targets and highlight some lessons learned.

Defining effectiveness of health targets

As noted above, the evaluation of health targets is straightforward at one level. Since health targets incorporate specific, measurable and time-bound objectives, they provide their own mechanisms for evaluation. From this perspective, evaluation involves the collection of relevant data, together with the definition of an appropriate time frame and the parameters that define success or failure. The extent to which a target has been achieved is thus expressed as:

$$\textit{Target achievement (\%)} = \frac{100 \text{ current value} - \textit{baseline}}{\textit{target year (year X)} - \textit{baseline}}$$

The resulting percentage may then be transformed into ordinal categories such as achieved (= 100%), partially achieved (e.g. 50%-99%) and not achieved (<50%). Several countries and subnational entities use such an approach for evaluating their health targets, as illustrated by the cases from Catalonia, England and France. The United States of America and the Netherlands use this approach but are not described in this volume.

Such technocratic evaluations are clearly an essential element of any strategy that incorporates health targets. Yet, at best, they are an incomplete evaluation of the use of targets. Instead it is necessary to look at whether the use of targets led to the overall outcomes for the health system anticipated when a targets-based approach was chosen. In essence, two important questions must be addressed. What should be evaluated? What outcomes are health targets meant to achieve?

At least three foci can be selected for the first question: the success (however measured) of the policy of employing health targets (e.g. does it improve the governance of the health system?); the impact of individual targets on the achievement of desired outcomes; and whether the specific targets have been achieved (even if opportunistic behaviour means that the broader goals are undermined). If they evaluate at all, many countries concentrate on the last of these – the technocratic perspective described above. If the target is to lower the mortality of a given disease by 10% within 10 years, they evaluate whether the mortality actually is 10% lower after this time. However, this is only a partial evaluation of the strategy within which the target is embedded and has been criticized on two counts.

First, if a target is not achieved it is easily dismissed as "too ambitious". If it is achieved it may be dismissed because "it would have been reached anyway". These statements deserve closer examination. The former requires a thorough knowledge of the potential effect sizes (efficacy) of various intervention strategies and the possible combinations of interventions. The latter assumes that longitudinal trends remain constant over time. This may not be the case.

Life expectancy in the Russian Federation provides a useful example. If, in 1991, a target had been set to keep life expectancy constant until 2000, this could have been criticized as likely to have been achieved anyway. If the resulting policies had managed to half the actual decline observed it is now clear that this would have been a partial success, even though most evaluations would label it a failure. The converse also holds true. Experts may judge a target to be neither overambitious nor trivial. However, it is often impossible to know whether success can be attributed to the policies pursued. It is difficult to differentiate the contributions made by different influences, given the many factors that affect health (Busse 1999).

This leads to the second question. What are the desired outcomes of health targets? From the technocratic-epidemiological view, the fundamental purpose of health targets is to improve population health. Yet, as stated earlier, changes in population health can take a long time. Thus, data on outcomes must be supplemented by appropriate measures of process that are known to predict eventual outcomes. One obvious example is the use of prevalence of smokers as a predictor of later deaths from lung cancer. However, these measures are only a limited subset of the legitimate goals of a target-based strategy. The process of developing such a strategy may lead to less tangible outcomes that provide the basis for sustained health improvement. Examples include the creation of alliances dedicated to achieving better health or engaging actors from other sectors in the promotion of health. Assessment of these aspects of a target-based strategy requires qualitative methods to supplement the quantitative assessment of the targets themselves. Based on these assessments, some general lessons can be learned.

Health targets: what works and what does not; what can be done

Approaches to achieving health targets

The case studies demonstrate two different approaches to the use of targets. The first seeks to change behaviour through regulation. This involves the creation of an accountability framework, backed by a combination of sanctions and incentives and implemented through a monitoring system. The second approach is based on consensus, backed by financial incentives. This seeks to create ownership by involving all relevant stakeholders. Earmarked financing is key to effecting the behaviour change that will achieve the desired outcomes.

England provides an example of the regulatory approach. A strong accountability framework, backed up by intensive monitoring, is designed to achieve compliance at all levels of the NHS. Targets are incorporated in quasi-contracts (PSAs), in which funds are linked to achievement (HM Treasury 1999). At an organizational level, the salaries of senior managers are linked to achievement of targets. There are also sanctions for failure – a senior manager who fails to hit targets consistently can expect to be replaced. This has led to a situation where there is a high turnover of senior managers, with a resulting loss of institutional memory and an aversion to risk taking (HM Treasury 1999).

The consensus approach is seen in Flanders and France, where financial incentives were provided to support the achievement of targets. In Flanders, for example, the school fruit programme brought together local government, fruit suppliers and schools. Local government provided logistical and financial support and local health networks (LHNs) provided educational materials. The French Cancer Plan involved total funding of €640 million up to 2007 and the creation of 3900 jobs.

Whichever approach is adopted, three elements are important for success – accountability, participation and adequate funding. No one appears to have achieved complete success so far but some elements seem to be necessary for at least limited success. It is clear that many administrations have attempted to embark on target-based programmes without putting in place the mechanisms necessary to bring about change. Some of these countries relied solely on achieving ownership and consensus, without resources or accountability. Others put in place resources and accountability but failed to achieve ownership. These requirements are now examined in more detail.

Accountability

Good governance requires those responsible for implementing policies to account for their actions. In turn, the accountability framework in which they work should be transparent and based on established rules and regulations. In other words, they should be held responsible for achieving policy goals that are explicit and set out in advance. They should not be held responsible for failing to implement policies that are unclear, vague or otherwise inadequately specified, or where the system of rules and regulations denies them any mechanisms by which they can actually be implemented. Catalonia (Spain), Flanders (Belgium) and France each provide examples of different models of accountability frameworks.

In Catalonia, the legislature (regional parliament) played a major role in endorsing targets. It received public progress reports from the executive branch of government and elicited accountability from those charged with implementation by its ability to withhold financial incentives, backed up by publication of performance. This system was introduced within the permissive legal framework established by the Spanish health act, which devolved responsibility for health policy to the regions. Coordination was facilitated by the creation of an interregional committee (see Chapter 5).

France has also adopted a system of accountability where the executive reports to the legislature. The Act on Public Health Policy gives the executive responsibility for implementing health policy and in turn requires it to deliver a progress report to the National Assembly every five years (Wismar et al. 2006). Accountability flows down to the regional governments; these are required to develop health plans consistent with national targets (see Chapter 8).

In contrast, the Minister of Health in Flanders is formally responsible to the regional parliament for achievement of the health targets but the system of accountability is rather less clear.

In England, target setting is essentially confined to the executive, emerging from a dialogue between the Department (ministry) of Health and HM Treasury, with no meaningful involvement of the legislature. Parliament has only loose and very general oversight as those responsible for achievement of targets are accountable directly to ministers (Department of Health 2004). The publication of results could be seen to provide a degree of public accountability but it is not clear what sanctions are open to the public in the event of failure, given that those charged with the implementation of targets are unelected. The unchecked power of the executive means that targets can be changed frequently, with little explanation and little consideration of whether there are the resources necessary to achieve them. This may explain the numerous unintended consequences that arise.

In summary, the governance systems that give rise to health targets are largely a consequence of the constitutional and historical situations in each country. Those setting targets must take these into account and develop a system of ensuring accountability that is contextually relevant.

Participation

Participation is widely seen as an important element of good governance. It helps to build ownership of policies and ensures that potential pitfalls are identified in advance. By subjecting health targets (and the policies they stem from) to detailed discussion, it is less likely that mistakes will be made and more likely that they will reflect genuine health needs.

In Catalonia, consumer education and involvement encouraged stakeholder participation. Health councils were created at regional level and had popular representation, in the form of trade unions and citizen associations. These regional health councils had the authority to implement health-policy changes (see Chapter 5). The plan involved the participation and input of approximately 3000 people. This shift in policy-making involved a number of actors in developing a comprehensive strategy on target setting.

In Flanders, targets were implemented at the local level under the supervision of LHNs. These bodies were responsible for planning, implementing, registering and evaluating local prevention projects. Moreover, they played a central role in coordinating the participation of the actors necessary for programme delivery and served as a liaison for intra- and inter-sectoral collaboration (see Chapter 7).

The federal targets initiative in Germany achieved a high level of stakeholder participation. Over 70 institutions and 200 experts, as well as citizen and patient groups, provided important input to the process of target formation. Health targets supported coordination both within and between political levels and contributed to the development of an organizational framework for health-service provision. The regional governments (Länder) became proactive in defining health targets after the first federal initiative failed. They pressed the federal government to define national health targets and provide regional-level support to related activities. Despite these efforts, health targets have made little impression on popular consciousness (see Chapter 9).

In England, the pre-1997 government's public health strategy (Health of the Nation) involved a top-down approach. Some considered that this incorporated a predominantly medical view of health targets, with heavy reliance on health-service provision and little attention to broader influences on public health. Local engagement was sometimes problematic because a sense of ownership was lacking.

The available evidence suggests that targets face resistance at local level if they are imposed on those who must implement them. Mechanisms that foster participation and a sense of ownership are an important element of a target-based strategy.

Adequate funding

The importance of funding has been noted in relation to France's Cancer Plan and the Flemish school fruit programme. However, these are exceptions and, as the case studies reveal, often targets are not backed by adequate resources.

Funding is also required for supporting infrastructure. In England, it became clear that routinely available data were insufficient to allow monitoring of the progress of the Health of the Nation strategy. This led to the establishment of the annual Health Survey for England, widely seen as a model for what is required in order to draw meaningful comparisons of health within Europe. The authorities in Hungary also took action – in partnership with organizations from six counties, the Hungarian School of Public Health established the first regional health observatory in central and eastern Europe (see Chapter 10).

Lessons learned where success has been elusive

It is important to learn lessons from failures as well as successes. The authors of the Hungarian case study identify the lack of an accountability framework as a reason why target setting failed to achieve its objectives. Ten years after the first target-based health policies were initiated, there is still no system to hold anyone to account for their achievement (see Chapter 10). Monitoring was also deficient; the Hungarian health-monitoring system was incapable of providing information at the regional level, where many policies were implemented. The Hungarian policy was also hindered by a lack of ownership among those whose commitment was essential for success, both inside and outside the health sector. Health professionals exhibited a low level of awareness. An interministerial committee was established to engage those from other sectors but could achieve little in the absence of dedicated financial resources.

The Hungarian experience has some echoes in the Russian Federation. There, targets were politically driven and widely viewed as neither relevant nor necessary. Crucially, health was not seen as a political priority in either the Soviet Union or (subsequently) the Russian Federation. Those targets that were set were nonspecific and focused on inputs rather than outcomes. They rarely required any change in policy to achieve them (see Chapter 11). Later targets (from 1997) were more ambitious but produced few changes in the absence of budgetary support. Worse, the absence of an effective regulatory system led to opportunistic behaviour and creative accounting.

The failure of strategies based on health targets in the Russian Federation and Hungary was due, in part, to weak governance. However, targets in Germany were not met despite a strong system of governance. There was a high level of consensus around the federal target initiative, reflecting the large number and variety of stakeholders that participated in its formulation. Initiatives that involved more restricted ranges of stakeholders faced immediate problems with ownership and acceptability.

The major problems seen in Germany were the lack of accountability mechanisms and dedicated financing, and an inadequate monitoring system. Health targets were linked to the allocation of funds in only a few exceptional circumstances, even then funds were sometimes promised but never materialized. It was assumed that stakeholders would pursue the health targets voluntarily. Eventually, the federal government disengaged from the national health targets initiative and left it to the other stakeholders. The focus of target setting is now in the Länder.

Yet again, these findings emphasize that a target-based strategy is more likely to be effective if it is based on consensus and elicits ownership from those required to implement it. In Catalonia, health councils enabled citizen groups to take an active part in target setting. In Flanders, LHNs brought together key stakeholders with a role in promoting health. In France, consensus was established through a series of national and regional health conferences. In all of these examples, stakeholders had the opportunity to debate the health problems facing them, foster partnerships and identify responses. In contrast, there is little prospect of achieving success when targets are not based on consensus and ownership.

It is also clear that it is important to keep targets constantly under review and identify those that are either unrealistically challenging or too easy. In Flanders, the health targets established in 1998 were revised regularly, albeit in an ad hoc fashion; thereafter a formal mechanism was put in place to keep them updated. It is also important to review where responsibility lies. In Germany, the initiative shifted to the Länder after the apparent failure of a federal proposal for health targets. In turn this encouraged the federal authorities to reconsider national targets that could complement activities at the regional level.

Conclusion

It is clear that effective target programmes require investment (either financial or in systems that promote accountability and participation) over a long period and across many sectors, including the health sector itself. This important actor has been forgotten in the exercise of setting and implementing health targets and produced a situation in which such programmes have lain in the forgotten corner of health policy, i.e. as a topic for interested outsiders. "Real" health policy continues to concentrate on health services (Busse and Wismar 2002). This may seem understandable, given financial constraints, political adversity and political scepticism. Yet, given the substantial resources spent on health care, it seems somewhat perverse that so often little effort goes into assessing what it is seeking to achieve.

REFERENCES

Busse R (1999). Evaluation and outcomes of health targets. *Eurohealth* 5(3):12-13.

Busse R, Wismar M (2002). Health target programmes and health care services – any link? A conceptual and comparative study (part 1). *Health Policy,* 59(3):209-221.

Department of Health (2004). *Choosing health: making healthy choices easier.* London, Department of Health.

HM Treasury (1999). *Public services for the future: modernization, reform, accountability.* London, The Stationery Office.

Wismar M et al. (2006). Health targets and (good) governance. *EuroObserver,* 8(Spring):1-8.

Part 2

Country and Region Experiences

Chapter 5

Catalonia: Improved Intelligence and Accountability?

Ricard Tresserras, Pilar Brugulat

Introduction

With seven million inhabitants in the north-east of Spain, Catalonia has been an autonomous region since 1979. Target setting began about 15 years ago and has produced some positive results. This case study presents an historical overview followed by a description of the experience of implementing targets. The remaining sections assess the experience of defining targets, using them to exert influence and monitor progress. The concluding section draws lessons from the Catalan experience.

Emergence of health targets

The regional government has a high degree of autonomy in the development of policy on health-care delivery. The emergence of health targets as a core element of Catalan health policy originated in a combination of ideas from outside – in particular WHO's Health for All in the Year 2000 strategy (World Health Organization 1981; WHO Regional Office for Europe 1985) – and an internal impetus to articulate clearly the objectives of public health. From the outset, it harnessed a combination of technical innovation and strong political commitment, both based on a commitment to evaluation and an evidenced-based approach. It was embedded in a health strategy: the Health Plan for Catalonia. This emerged from a participative process that drew on the ideas of approximately 3000 people from all levels of the health sector, rather than being developed exclusively at the centre (Departament de Sanitat i Seguretat Social 1992).

The process began when key stakeholders recognized the need to reorient the health system and change the focus from productivity to health outcomes. This was influenced strongly by a number of international developments, in particular WHO's Health for All policy and the American Healthy People initiative, both of which were inspirational. Practical implementation was guided by important technical insights into how to quantify targets, drawn from experiences in countries and subnational entities such as Scotland, Northern Ireland, Wales, Canada, England and the United States of America (Salleras and Via 1992).

Unlike in other countries (such as England) target setting in Catalonia began in the health sector and was subsequently adopted elsewhere. Regional policies were required to comply with the Spanish General Health Act and were developed within its framework. An interregional committee (Consejo Interterritorial del Sistema Nacional de Salud), brought together representatives from all Spanish regions and provided for nationwide coordination and learning from shared experience (Salleras et al. 1994).

The resulting Catalan Health Act introduced a split between financing and the provision of health care in Catalonia. This was at a time when the political climate was conducive to major reforms and produced a situation unlike that in the rest of Spain. The act was based on a series of explicit values, including equity, accessibility, effectiveness, quality and user satisfaction. These underpinned the target programme (now driven by the Catalan Health Service) but, in reality, most targets focused on effectiveness.

A Catalan Health Service was established as a purchasing organization within the Department of Health with responsibility for funding, contracting and operational planning. Health care was provided by a mix of public and private organizations. The public provider, the Catalan Institute of Health, delivered 80% of primary health-care services and 30% of hospital care.

The Catalan Department of Health periodically reported its intentions to the regional parliament in the form of a health plan. This did not require formal approval from the assembly, rather it set out the Minister of Health's commitment to achieve certain targets within a given period. The first edition was published in 1991, this Framework Document for the Elaboration of the Health Plan for Catalonia (Departament de Sanitat i Seguretat Social 1991) provided the basis for subsequent plans. Currently, two types of document are published. A strategic document is issued every ten years and supplemented by plans that give more emphasis to operational aspects, published every three to four years. The health plans report on progress towards the targets set out in previous plans. A major evaluation is conducted prior to the publication of each strategic plan (Departament de Sanitat i Seguretat Social 1991; Departament de Sanitat i Seguretat Social 2003; Departament de Sanitat i Seguretat Social 1992; Departament de Sanitat i Seguretat Social 1997; Departament de Sanitat i Seguretat Social 1999).

Generating targets

The selection of initial targets involved an extensive process of consultation. Teams sought to identify priority areas, link priorities to measurable indicators, determine the expected time needed to achieve a target, and finally, to operationalize the targets agreed. The overall goal was: "adding life to years and adding health to life."

A three-stage process was used to define the targets. First, identification of the leading health problems (assessed by burden of disease) that were amenable to interventions was undertaken and targets were set to improve their outcomes. Second, specification of the associated risk factors was made and the targets necessary to reduce them. Third, operational targets linked to the processes required to achieve the first two sets of targets were set. As far as possible, the formulation of targets included evidence on baseline levels, the direction and magnitude of the expected change, time over which it should be achieved and the indicators to be used for evaluation. The WHO Regional Office for Europe's targets were used extensively. Specific goals were defined where either WHO targets had not been set or they had been achieved in Catalonia (Salleras et al. 1994; Tresserras et al. 2000).

The initial set of targets focused on health outcomes rather than processes, even though the target-setting initiative had emerged within a context of health-system reform. In the first planning period (until 2000) 19 health problems were identified as priorities, involving 22 sets of interventions.

Of course, it is important that targets engage those who will be responsible for achieving them. The initial period was characterized by enthusiasm and active participation among health professionals who welcomed the commitment to a stronger evidence base for the ongoing health-care reforms. This was followed by a period of growing scepticism, in part reflecting methodological difficulties in setting and operationalizing targets. At this point, some professionals considered this a fruitless exercise with little chance of success. An evaluation of target setting occurred in the third period. Targets were seen as a way of reorienting health policies and services, although it was accepted that improved methods were needed. However, those working in the health sector did see the target-based approach as a way of making their needs more visible and a useful means to identify priorities.

The evaluation of the target-based system in 2000 was an important step that contributed to the credibility, transparency and legitimacy of this element of health-policy development (Salleras and Tresserras 2003; Tresserras et al. 2000). The evaluation identified a number of weaknesses in the initial targets. For example, not all dimensions were included; those that were were not well-developed. There was little attention to equity, accessibility, quality or satisfaction and greater emphasis was placed on the aggregate level of health indicators rather than their distribution, according to social class, territorial units or gender.

Accountability

Accountability was a key element of the target-based model and the Health Plan of Catalonia elicited a high level of professional participation. Details were widely disseminated and available on the Department of Health's web site, thus seeking to ensure a high level of transparency.

As noted earlier, each health plan is presented to the Catalan parliament. Although it is not required to grant approval, the Catalan Minister of Health is held accountable for accomplishment of the activities and achievement of the targets. Reporting is straightforward as most of the targets are quantitative, with a defined time horizon and links to a specific indicator. Thus (at least in theory), there is an effective mechanism to ensure transparency and accountability to the public and to parliament.

In practice, the outcomes of the health plans have not been subject to parliamentary scrutiny. No activity was elicited when the 2000 evaluation was presented to parliament – the opposition did not use its right to ask the government whether or not the targets had been achieved. A formal requirement for parliament to approve the health plans and scrutinize achievements could provide for a more enriching debate and even provoke a greater degree of political commitment to the policies pursued. The development of a cross-party consensus might also facilitate the adoption of policies that extend beyond a political mandate.

The question of accountability raises other issues. The diverse determinants of health mean that any strategy must take a multisectoral approach – the health sector can provide leadership but it must engage with other sectors. However, there is no mechanism to judge their contributions to overall health gain. Examples included targets to reduce injuries associated with traffic and domestic violence against women. How to strengthen this wider accountability is a subject of continuing debate.

Collecting and using intelligence

The target-setting process led to a significant reappraisal of the use of health data, previously a low priority. In 2001, a systematic review was undertaken to map the availability of routine sources that were relevant to the targets and thus identify where new data-collection systems were needed.

Table 5-1 *Sources of data for monitoring targets*

Existing data	Ad hoc studies
Population census	Catalan Health Survey
Mortality data	Catalan Health Examination Survey
Hospital discharge data	Survey of smoking amongst professionals (physicians, nurses, teachers, pharmacists)
Infectious disease notifications	
Drug use	Child dental survey
Maternal and child health care	Physical activity survey
Workplace injuries	Drug consumption survey
Assisted reproduction	Evaluation of the use of preventive practises in primary health care by auditing clinical records
Abortion	Catalan Nutritional Survey
Renal disease	Nosocomial infections register
	Girona Heart Registry (REGICOR)

Girona Heart Registry (REGICOR)

The Department of Health published an official report of the health plan evaluation and 25 papers were published in the highly reputed Spanish scientific journal Medicina Clínica (Salleras and Tresserras 2003). Moreover, most of the data used to undertake the evaluation were available to the public. Yet, there was very little interest in the evaluation at either political or technical levels despite these considerable efforts to make the relevant information available.

The evaluation highlighted the existing data's emphasis on processes rather than evaluations of health outcomes. For example, the evaluation of primary health-care settings gave more attention to controlling risk factors rather than addressing health problems such as pneumonia. In particular, the evaluation highlighted the limited information on lifestyles and health determinants. This led to the creation of a public health agency to address behavioural issues.

Outcomes

There has been a mixed experience of implementing targets in Catalonia. Some positive results include a more explicit articulation of public health goals; strengthened evidence base for policy-making; and strengthened public participation in health policy. However, it is more difficult to identify gains in health outcomes or resource allocation. Similarly, although the use of targets has strengthened accountability, there is still much to do to improve monitoring and performance management. Box 5-1 gives examples of targets and progress towards them.

The most positive benefits could be seen in the policy process. Targets became integrated into the Department of Health's activities at both political and technical levels. This contributed to a more rational approach to health policies that has evolved positively in recent years. It can be seen in improved definition and prioritization of key health problems, and in the development of plans to tackle them. This process was increasingly underpinned by a systematic analysis of epidemiological data on the health status of the Catalan population.

There had been little public participation in health policy in Catalonia but this changed when the Catalan Health Service created health councils at regional and local levels. These included representatives from the public (trade unions,

Box 5-1 *Selected targets from the Catalan experience*

Health outcome targets	Result	Risk reduction targets	Result
Reduce cancer mortality rates <65 yrs (by 15%)	Achieved	Reduce smoking prevalence >14 yrs (by 20%); 15-24 yrs (by 18%)	Not achieved
Stabilize mortality rates of breast cancer and lung cancer	Achieved	Increase proportion of smoking cessation >14 yrs (by 30%).	Achieved
Reduce cervical cancer mortality rates (by 25%)	Partially achieved	Increase prevalence of adults who walk more than 30 minutes per day (by 50%)	Not achieved
		Reduce prevalence of people who are sedentary during leisure (by 40%)	Partially achieved

Note: Achieved – change in the indicator equal to, or greater than, expected. Partially achieved – more than 50% of the expected change. Not achieved – less than 50% of the expected change.

citizen associations, patient associations) and health sectors (health professionals). Overall health plans were subject to approval by the Catalan and regional health councils; more specific policies that acted over shorter periods also incorporated public involvement. However, the process of public involvement is challenging. Further efforts are underway to strengthen this, including greater use of the Internet, better documentation, focus groups and health surveys.

More mixed results were achieved in the pursuit of health gain. This assessment is complicated by the absence of a control group as it is impossible to know what would have happened in the absence of a target-based strategy. However, the process was beneficial because it strengthened the culture of evaluation.

An evaluation of the health plan targets for 2000 showed that most of the health-related targets were achieved. An increase in disability-free life expectancy was observed and there were positive trends in the major measures of mortality. A total of 106 targets were evaluated, of these the majority – 68 (64.1%) were fully achieved; 9 (8.5%) were partially achieved; and 29 (27.4%) were not achieved. Success was more likely where targets related to the delivery of health services; those focused on public health issues were less likely to be successful. Five targets could not be evaluated because they had been formulated poorly or the data required could not be obtained without disproportionate cost.

There is limited evidence that targets had an effect on the allocation of resources. This may be because the predominant focus on health outcomes made it difficult for managers to see the link between their own activities and the achievement of improved health outcomes at a population level. Furthermore, there were no financial incentives to achieve targets. More recent efforts to link budgets to the achievement of targets have been a learning process and it remains difficult to define this linkage. Recently developed steering plans linked to budgetary allocations may be the answer. These focus on a small number of health problems, with closely specified targets designed to achieve high-quality services in all parts of the Catalan Health Service. At present they focus on mental health, cancer, cardiovascular disease, ageing and the health of the immigrant population.

Lessons learned

Target setting in Catalonia has not been a straightforward process but significant progress has been achieved, going beyond the aspirational to actual implementation. The Catalan experience provides a number of lessons on how to incorporate targets into a health-policy framework and where improvements are needed. More than ten years of experience in setting targets and developing health plans have taught the main lessons listed below.

It is difficult to tackle inequalities. Few data are available to assess the health status of disadvantaged groups, or even according to more simple variables such as sex, social class or territorial units. Considerable strengthening of existing information systems is needed.

The Health Plan for Catalonia explicitly emphasized primary health care, seeking to redress the traditional emphasis on the hospital sector. However, no one part of the health system can be considered in isolation and targets should cover the entire health-care continuum where possible.

It has been very difficult to find the link between health targets and service delivery. Service contracts have not been sufficient, even when linked to targets. Other approaches that include guidelines and benchmarking are needed.

Intersectorality remains a major problem. The involvement of other sectors is essential but difficult, often depending more on personal capacities rather than institutional arrangements.

An integrated vision is necessary, requiring complementary action to change health services. This should embrace preventive, primary care; hospitals; intensive technology; and transportation of patients.

The involvement of health professionals is crucial. Much still needs to be done to extend knowledge and acceptance of the Health Plan for Catalonia and achieve shared ownership of its goals. Although there have been attempts to reach out to the population and involve them in the establishment of priorities, more work is needed to ensure active citizen participation.

Finally, an earmarked budget linked to the achievement of health targets would strengthen the capacity to influence health-policy development.

REFERENCES

Departament de Sanitat i Seguretat Social (1991). *Document marc per a l'elaboració del Pla de Salut de Catalunya [Framework document outlining the Health Plan for Catalonia]*, Barcelona, Generalitat de Catalunya (English version available at: http://www.gencat.net/salut/depsan/units/sanitat/pdf/index_1991.pdf. accessed 14 May 2008.

Departament de Sanitat i Seguretat Social (1992). *Pla de Salut de Catalunya 1993-1995 [Health plan for Catalonia 1993-1995]*. Barcelona, Generalitat de Catalunya (English version available at: http://www.gencat.net/salut/depsan/units/sanitat/html/ca/plasalut/pla1993.htm, accessed 14 May 2008.

Departament de Sanitat i Seguretat Social (1997). *Pla de Salut de Catalunya 1996-1998. [Health plan for Catalonia 1996-1998].* Barcelona, Generalitat de Catalunya (English version available at: http://www.gencat.net/salut/depsan/units/sanitat/pdf/pla19962.pdf, accessed 14 May 2008).

Departament de Sanitat i Seguretat Social (1999). *Pla de Salut de Catalunya 1999-2001. [Health plan for Catalonia 1999-2001].* Barcelona, Generalitat de Catalunya (English version available at: http://www.gencat.net/salut/depsan/units/sanitat/html/en/dir228/index.html, accessed 9 May 2008).

Departament de Sanitat i Seguretat Social (2003). *Estrategies de salut per a l'any 2010. Pla de Salut de Catalunya 2002-2005. [Strategies for health for the year 2010. Health plan for Catalonia 2002-2005].* Barcelona, Generalitat de Catalunya (English version available at: http://www.gencat.net/salut/depsan/units/sanitat/html/en/dir228/index.html .

Salleras L et al. (1994). *Working together for health gain at regional level. The experience of Catalonia.* Barcelona, Generalitat de Catalunya.

Salleras L, Tresserras R (2003). Evaluación de los objetivos de salud y disminución de riesgo del Plan de Salud de Cataluña para el año 2000. [Evaluation of the objectives of health and examination of the risks in the Health Plan of Catalonia for the year 2000]. *Med Clin (Barc),* 121(Suppl 1):1-142 (English version available at:http://www.gencat.net/salut/depsan/units/sanitat/html/en/dir228/index.html).

Salleras L, Via JM (1992). Setting targets for health policy; the Catalonian approach. In: Ritsatakis A, ed. *The process for health policy development. Report of a working group on the development of subnational policies for health.* Copenhagen, WHO Regional Office for Europe: 51-82.

Tresserras R, Castell C, Salleras L (2000). Development of a policy for health for all in Catalonia. In: Ritsatakis BR et al., eds. *Exploring health policy development in Europe.* Copenhagen, WHO Regional Office for Europe (WHO Regional Publications, European Series, No. 86).

Tresserras R et al. (2000). Health targets and priorities in Catalonia, Spain. *European Journal of Public Health,* 10(Suppl. 4):51-56.

WHO Regional Office for Europe (1981). *European regional strategy for attaining health for all.* Copenhagen, WHO Regional Office for Europe (EUR/RC30/8 Rev. 2).

WHO Regional Office for Europe (1985). *Targets for Health for All. Targets in support of the European regional strategy for health for all.* Copenhagen, WHO Regional Office for Europe.

Chapter 6

England: Intended and Unintended Effects

Peter C. Smith[2]

Introduction

To many observers, the English NHS appears to be the archetypal planned health system and it would be natural to assume that targets have been a central feature since its inception in 1948. However, this is not the case. In the early years of the NHS, the health system was dominated by the largely autonomous actions of health-care professionals, especially doctors. The only meaningful target under which local health-care organizations operated was the requirement to work within a fixed annual budget. Indeed, even this requirement was implemented flexibly. Often, local institutions (such as hospitals) were able to breach budgetary limits providing that the aggregate NHS budget was adhered to across the system as a whole.[3]

Traditionally, the gatekeeping role of general practitioners (GPs) has made an important contribution to cost control. Every citizen must be registered with a GP and access to non-emergency specialist care can be secured only by a GP referral. Compared with their counterparts in other developed countries, British GPs have shown a high level of restraint in making such referrals. The other major mechanism for securing adherence to budgetary limits has been the waiting list, for both inpatient and outpatient treatment. Waiting times have been a striking and persistent feature of the NHS; historically much longer than in other developed countries (Martin and Smith 1999). Demand from those wanting to avoid waiting has led to a small but significant private

[2] The preparation of this chapter was supported by Economic and Social Research Council research fellowship R000271253.

[3] Primary care is an important area of expenditure that initially was not subject to the same budgetary limits.

health-care market funded through private insurance or out-of-pocket payments. This accounts for about 15% of non-emergency surgery.

Historically, the system exhibited very strong cost control but little coherence or any evidence of planning. Moreover, as international comparisons became available in the 1990s, it also became apparent that the quality of health care offered by the NHS was inferior to that in many other mature health systems (Wanless 2002). Targets were announced occasionally but they appear to have been largely ignored. No meaningful strategies for securing these targets were implemented until the 1990s.

Attempts to seek to impose more coherence and managerial control over the NHS began in the mid-1980s, with the introduction of general management. Non-clinical managers were introduced into local health authorities in an attempt to ensure that resources were allocated more rationally, in line with the national policy for the NHS. Although this scheme appeared to have only limited impact, it paved the way for more radical reforms (Klein 1995). In 1991, the Thatcher government abandoned the traditional arrangements under which local health authorities acted as both payers and providers of local health services. The purchasing functions were retained by local health authorities, but public providers (most especially NHS hospitals) were now expected to compete for business from health authorities in an internal market for health care.[4] Although some reference was made to quality improvement, the main objective of the internal market was to secure efficiency improvements in the form of reduced unit costs. In practice, the market was heavily regulated and researchers have found it difficult to find any major change in health-system behaviour that is directly attributable to its implementation (Le Grand et al. 1998).

The incoming Labour government of 1997 announced the creation of a new NHS but initially left many of the existing structures in place – most particularly the internal market (Smith and Goddard 2000). The performance of the NHS failed to change perceptibly and there arose a belief that the low levels of funding of English health care were contributing to poor clinical outcomes. In 1999, the Prime Minister agreed to a major increase in NHS funding, conditional on the introduction of a much tougher performance-management regime. The outcome was the NHS Plan (2000), a ten-year vision for the NHS that contained a plethora of over 400 detailed objectives (Department of Health 2000).

---

[4] Also, general practices could elect to become fundholders — using budgets delegated by health authorities to purchase routine specialist procedures. By 1997, when the scheme was abolished, over 50% of patients were registered with a fundholding general practice.

This chapter traces the growing role of targets within the NHS. The first tentative steps were taken in the public health domain and these are described first. Targets have also become a central feature of health-care delivery. This started modestly with The Patient's Charter in 1991 but targets have become a central feature of English public services (not least the NHS) since the election of Tony Blair in 1997. More recent developments include a system of performance ratings for all NHS organizations and an ambitious new contract for GPs. Both of these embody important health-care targets and are described below. A concluding section draws some general inferences from the English experience.

Targets for public health

The Health of the Nation was the first concerted attempt to introduce targets into English public health (Department of Health 1992). Launched in 1992, it owed a heavy debt to WHO's Health for All initiative. However, the strategy was also attributable to the creation of the NHS internal market. Health authorities became purchasers of health care, and were freed from a preoccupation with its delivery. The intention was that they should therefore focus more single-mindedly on what they were purchasing – the health of their population. Health of the Nation can be seen as an attempt to set the public health agenda for local health authorities in the reformed NHS.

The initial strategy selected five key areas for action:

1. coronary heart disease and stroke
2. cancers
3. mental illness
4. HIV/AIDS and sexual health
5. accidents.

A small number of national targets were specified for each key area. For example, the first key area had three targets.

1. To reduce death rates for both coronary heart disease (CHD) and stroke in people under 65 by at least 40% by the year 2000.
2. To reduce the death rate for CHD in people aged 65-74 by at least 30% by the year 2000.
3. To reduce the death rate for stroke in people aged 65-74 by at least 40% by the year 2000.

A total of 15 such targets were set, each with 1990 as the base year. A further set of 10 risk factor targets was specified in order to make them operational, covering smoking, diet and nutrition, blood pressure and drug misuse. A full epidemiological analysis accompanied the Health of the Nation strategy and a detailed implementation strategy was specified.

The Health of the Nation was England's first attempt to put in place a systematic public health strategy. It was widely welcomed and embodied many of the principles promoted in Health for All. However, it is noteworthy that as its development was driven principally by public health professionals it produced a predominantly medical view of health targets (Hunter 2002). The health service was seen as the chief instrument for securing health improvement, with little attention to broader influences on public health. In one sense this was reasonable as it sought to influence the actions of health authorities. On the other hand, it missed the opportunity to engage a broader coalition of actors capable of influencing health outcomes, for example those in the voluntary sector, other local public services and national ministries.

A careful independent evaluation in 1998 concluded that its "impact on policy documents peaked as early as 1993; and, by 1997, its impact on local policymaking was negligible" (Department of Health 1998). Put simply, health authorities felt they had more pressing concerns than public health. They concentrated on operational issues, such as reducing waiting times and securing budgetary control. The evaluation concluded that the high-level national targets did not resonate with local decision-makers. "National targets were a useful rallying point, but the encouragement to develop local targets would have been welcomed within the national framework as a reflection of local needs." There was also seen to be a lack of incentives and institutional capacity for local managers.

Hunter (2002) summarizes the weaknesses of the Health of the Nation strategy under six broad headings.

1. There appeared to be a lack of leadership in the national government.
2. The policy failed to address the underlying social and structural determinants of health.
3. The targets were not always credible, and were not formulated at a local level.
4. There was poor communication of the strategy beyond the health system.
5. The strategy was not sustained.
6. Partnership between agencies was not encouraged.

The overarching message was that the strategy and its associated targets did not permeate the health system strongly enough to make a material difference.

Following the 1997 election of the Blair government, in 1998 the Health of the Nation was replaced with a new public health strategy – Saving Lives: Our Healthier Nation. This had the objective of improving healthy life expectancy of all citizens (especially the most disadvantaged) by focusing attention on health inequalities. In other respects it retained many of the characteristics of its predecessor but it was soon subsumed into a broader health-system targets regime. This was initiated in the development of the NHS Plan in 2000, described in more detail below. Hunter (Hunter 2002) gives a fuller treatment of English public health targets.

Targets for health-service delivery

Alongside the public health targets, successive British governments have sought to introduce targets specifically within health care. The first initiative was The Patient's Charter, introduced in 1991 (Department of Health 1991). This sought to guarantee certain minimum health-care standards within the NHS, many of which were not especially challenging. For example, the standards on "access to services" included the right to:

- have any proposed treatment, including any risks involved in that treatment and any alternatives, clearly explained to you before you decide whether to agree to it;

- have access to your health records, and to know that everyone working for the NHS is under a legal duty to keep your records confidential;

- have any complaint about NHS services (whoever provides them) investigated and to get a quick, full written reply from the relevant chief executive or general manager within four weeks;

- receive detailed information on local health services, this includes information on the standards of service you can expect, waiting times and on local GP services.

The major innovation was a guaranteed maximum waiting time for non-emergency surgery – 2 years in the first instance but reduced to 18 months by 1995. The Patient's Charter succeeded in eliminating very long waits in the NHS, these had been comparatively few but politically important. However, the incoming Labour government of 1997 was elected on a promise to reduce the size of NHS waiting lists rather than the length of waiting times. Having abandoned the Charter, for some time they struggled to find an alternative instrument for controlling waiting times that began to increase again.[5]

Meanwhile, the national government was developing important new initiatives for public service management. From 1998, the finance ministry (HM Treasury)

---

[5] It soon became clear that the size of NHS waiting lists was not a sensible focus of policy attention, government attention soon reverted to waiting times.

set the health ministry (Department of Health) challenging strategic targets in the form of public service agreements (PSAs), in common with all other government departments (HM Treasury 1999). One of their distinctive features

Box 6-1 *Sample of Department of Health PSA targets, 2004, for objective 1*

Objective I: Improve the health of the population. By 2010 increase life expectancy at birth in England to 78.6 years for men and to 82.5 years for women.

1.   Substantially reduce mortality rates by 2010:

- from heart disease and stroke and related diseases by at least 40% in people under 75, with at least a 40% reduction in the inequalities gap between the fifth of areas with the worst health and deprivation indicators and the population as a whole;
- from cancer by at least 20% in people under 75, with a reduction in the inequalities gap of at least 6% between the fifth of areas with the worst health and deprivation indicators and the population as a whole; and
- from suicide and undetermined injury by at least 20%.

2.   Reduce health inequalities by 10% by 2010 as measured by infant mortality and life expectancy at birth.

3.   Tackle the underlying determinants of ill health and health inequalities by:

- reducing adult smoking rates to 21% or less by 2010, with a reduction in prevalence among routine and manual groups to 26% or less;
- halting the year-on-year rise in obesity among children under 11 by 2010 in the context of a broader strategy to tackle obesity in the population as a whole; and
- reduce the under-18 conception rate by 50% by 2010 as part of a broader strategy to improve sexual health.

Standards

- A four hour maximum wait in Accident and Emergency from arrival to admission, transfer or discharge.
- Guaranteed access to a primary care professional within 24 hours and to a primary care doctor within 48 hours.
- Every hospital appointment booked for the convenience of the patient, making it easier for patients and their GPs to choose the hospital and consultant that best meets their needs.
- Improve life outcomes of adults and children with mental-health problems by ensuring that all patients who need them have access to crisis services and a comprehensive Child and Adolescent Mental Health Service.

Source: HM Treasury, 2004

is a focus on outcomes rather than operational activities of public service delivery. The 2004 PSAs for the health department are based on four broad objectives.

1. Improve the health of the population. By 2010, increase life expectancy at birth in England to 78.6 years for men and to 82.5 years for women.
2. Improve health outcomes for people with long-term conditions.
3. Improve access to services, in particular waiting times.
4. Improve the patient and user experience.

A sample of the detailed targets associated with objective 1 is given in Box 6-1. A set of even more detailed technical notes accompanies the targets. Four standards that must be maintained are listed at the bottom of the box. These reflect targets secured through previous PSAs that must continue to be achieved (HM Treasury 2004).

One of the Department of Health's key roles was to devise operational instruments to secure these targets. To this end, a crucial outcome of the NHS Plan was the development of a system of performance ratings. Individual NHS organizations (purchaser or provider of care) were ranked on a four-point scale (zero to three stars) according to a series of about 40 performance indicators. These were intended directly to reflect the objectives of the NHS, as embodied in the national PSAs (Department of Health 2001).

For each NHS organization, the indicators were combined according to a complex algorithm to produce the performance rating. The most important determinant of an organization's rating was its performance against a set of about 10 key indicators, dominated by measures of various aspects of patient waiting. This was augmented by a composite measure of performance based on a series of about 30 subsidiary indicators, combined in the form of a balanced scorecard view of the organization. Clinical quality comprised only a small element of the calculation. Subsequent ratings were prepared by a new health-care regulator – the Healthcare Commission. The performance indicators used to determine its ratings of acute hospitals in 2004 are shown in Table 6-1 overleaf (Healthcare Commission 2004). Whilst retaining the principle of performance ratings, it is noteworthy that the Commission implemented a major change to the assessment regime in 2006. This pays more attention to a broader spectrum of performance, most notably clinical quality (Healthcare Commission 2005).

Compared to previous target regimes, the most striking innovation associated with performance ratings was the introduction of strong managerial incentives dependent on the level of attainment (Hood and Bevan 2005). These included financial rewards, such as unfettered access to a performance fund, and some

Table 6-1 *Indicators for constructing performance ratings for acute hospitals, 2003-4*

Key targets	
12 hour wait standard for emergency inpatient admission Two week wait for first appointment for suspected cancer Achieving financial balance Satisfactory hospital cleanliness Improving working lives of staff Achieving targets for booking outpatient and elective appointments Outpatient waiting standards (21 weeks reducing to 17 weeks over course of the year) Non-emergency inpatient waiting standards (12 months reducing to 9 months over course of the year) Accident and Emergency wait of 4 hours or less	
Balanced scorecard indicators	
Clinical focus	child protection
	clinical governance composite indicator
	clinical negligence
	composite of participation in clinical audits
	deaths following heart bypass operations
	deaths following selected non-elective surgical procedures
	emergency readmission following discharge (adults)
	emergency readmission following discharge for a fractured hip
	indicator on stroke care
	infection control
	thrombolysis - < 30 minute door to needle time
	infection control
Patient focus	A&E emergency admission waits (<4 hours)
	adult inpatient and young patient surveys: access and waiting
	adult inpatient and young patient surveys: better information, more choice
	adult inpatient and young patient surveys: building closer relationships
	adult inpatient and young patient surveys: clean, comfortable, friendly place to be
	adult inpatient and young patient surveys: safe, high-quality, coordinated care
	better hospital food
	breast cancer: < 1 month diagnosis to treatment
	breast cancer: < 2 month GP urgent referral to treatment
	cancelled operations
	day case patient booking
	delayed transfers of care

Patient focus	delayed transfers of care
	patient complaints
	patients waiting longer than standard for revascularization
	< 6 month inpatient waits
	< 13 week outpatient waits
Capacity and capability	implementing specialist appraisal
	data quality on patient ethnic groups
	information governance
	junior doctors' hours
	staff opinion survey: health, safety and incidents
	staff opinion survey: human resource management
	staff opinion survey: staff attitudes

Source: Healthcare Commission web site

element of increased organizational autonomy. The jobs of senior executives of poorly performing organizations came under severe threat, and the performance indicators (especially the key targets) became a prime focus of managerial attention. More recently, the best performers in the acute hospital sector became eligible to apply for foundation status, implying considerably greater autonomy from direct NHS control.

Managers have had mixed responses to performance ratings. Many have criticized the system because of some apparently arbitrary ways in which the ratings are calculated, and their sensitivity to small data fluctuations (Barker et al. 2004). However, some acknowledge that the system gives better focus and a real lever with which to affect organizational behaviour and clinical practice. Reaction amongst health-care professionals has been less ambiguous. There is a widespread view that performance ratings distort clinical priorities and undermine professional autonomy (Mannion et al. 2005). This is hardly surprising, as one of the particular aims of the targets was to challenge traditional clinical behaviour and direct more attention to issues that had not always been a high priority, such as waiting times.

However, there is no doubt that performance ratings have delivered major improvements in the aspects of NHS care that they targeted (Bevan and Hood 2006). For example, the longest inpatient waiting times (a prime focus of the regime) have been rapidly eliminated (see Figure 6-1). Moreover, targeted aspects of English health care have improved markedly in comparison with Wales and Scotland. These two countries have higher funding levels but have not implemented performance ratings (Hauck and Street 2004).

Figure 6-1 *Trends in inpatient waiting lists in England, 1995-2004*

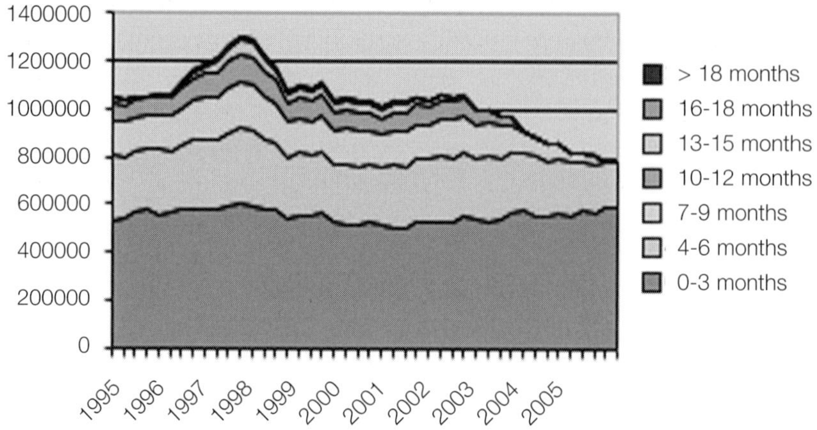

Source: Department of Health

Many commentators have criticized the English targets culture, a key issue of political debate across all public services. Alongside the manifest intended improvements in the measured targets there are widespread reports of adverse side-effects in other, often unmeasured, aspects of the health system (Bevan and Hood 2006). Many of these reports are anecdotal and may be apocryphal, but some have been credibly documented by the Public Administration Select Committee (House of Commons Public Administration Select Committee 2003). Examples include distorted behaviour (e.g. refusing to admit patients to accident departments until a four hour waiting-time target was achievable); ineffective responses (employing "hello nurses" to ensure that all accident patients were seen within 15 minutes); and fraud (manipulation of waiting lists).

It is noteworthy that the high-level PSAs include important public health targets under objective 1, including improved reduced-mortality rates from heart disease and cancer; reductions of health inequalities; and reduced rates of smoking, childhood obesity and teenage pregnancy. However, these high-level targets were not translated into meaningful local targets through the medium of the performance ratings system and therefore have not been the subject of as much sustained managerial attention as the health-service delivery targets (Marks and Hunter 2005).

There is growing concern that managers are concentrating on targeted and readily managed aspects of health care (most notably waiting times) at the expense of less controllable and less immediate concerns, such as public health. Hauck et al. (2003) show why this may have been the case. They examined 14 indicators of performance in English health care and sought to quantify the proportion of the variability in each indicator attributable to NHS regions,

NHS districts (nested within regions) and small areas (electoral wards). The results (summarized in Figure 6-2) show that variation in some indicators (most notably population mortality rates) seems to be largely beyond the control of health authorities. Up to 80% of other indicators (such as waiting time for surgery) are attributable to the actions of the health system. They concluded that managers confronted with equal rewards for both types of target are much more likely to expend effort on the areas over which they appear to have most control.

Unintended and adverse responses such as these were readily predictable from the Soviet literature (Nove 1980). They offer a powerful caution against sole reliance on a targets regime to secure improvement, and demonstrate the need

Figure 6-2 *Proportion of variability in performance indicators attributable to regional and district health authorities (intra-class correlation coefficients)*

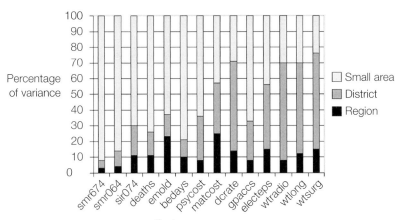

Key:

smr674	Standardized mortality ratio for ages 65-74
smr064	Standardized mortality ratio for ages 0-64
bedays	Length of stay
deaths	Deaths following hospital surgery (30 day perioperative mortality)
sir074	Limiting long-standing illness for ages 0-74
gpaccs	Accessibility to general practitioners
psycost	Psychiatry costs
emold	Emergency admissions of older people
matcost	Maternity costs per birth
electeps	Number of elective surgery episodes relative to expected
wtradio	Waiting time for radiotherapy
wtlong	Percentage of those on waiting list waiting for 12 months or more
dcrate	Day case rate
wtsurg	Waiting time for routine surgery

Source: Hauck et al. 2003

to put in countervailing instruments where necessary (Smith 1995). These might include a strong national data audit and surveillance capacity; a professional inspection system that monitors and reports on unintended consequences; careful scrutiny of performance beyond targets by organizational boards of governors; some sort of democratic voice in the control of local health organizations; and empowerment of patients through improved information and systems of redress.

It is noteworthy that the English Department of Health is aiming to correct the weaknesses of targets in the public health domain by putting in place an extensive range of very detailed operational initiatives that seek to promote public health objectives more specifically (Department of Health 2004). These seek to enable individuals to make healthier choices (using strategies such as better labelling of food) without entirely abandoning the role of more strategic and long-term targets (Adshead and Thorpe 2005).

Targets for GPs

Most GPs are independent practitioners who are contracted to provide specific services for the NHS. In 2004, a new contract implemented an ambitious system of quality targets and incentives (Department of Health 2003). About £ 1.3 billion, around 18% of GP income, is distributed annually on the basis of quality measures. The scheme has been developed in close negotiation with physicians, and was approved by 79.4% in a ballot of GPs, with a response rate of 70%.

In its initial form, the new incentive scheme used 146 quality indicators across 7 areas of practice. A certain number of quality points is available in each area, up to a maximum total of 1050 (Table 6-2). Around half of these are for clinical quality; other areas include practice organization (184 points) and

Table 6-2 GP contract: indicators and points at risk

Area of practice	Indicators	Points
Clinical	76	550
Organizational	56	184
Additional services	10	36
Patient experience	4	100
Holistic care (balanced clinical care)	–	100
Quality payments (balanced quality)	–	30
Access bonus	–	50
Maximum	146	1050

Table 6-3 *GP contract: clinical indicators*

Domain	Indicators	Points
Coronary heart disease including left ventricular dysfunction	15	121
Stroke or transient ischaemic attack	10	31
Cancer	2	12
Hypothyroidism	2	8
Diabetes	18	99
Hypertension	5	105
Mental health	5	41
Asthma	7	72
Chronic obstructive pulmonary disease	8	45
Epilepsy	4	16
Clinical maximum	76	550

Table 6-4 *Hypertension: indicators, scale and points at risk*

Records	Min	Max	Points
BP1 – practice can produce a register of patients with established hypertension	9		
Diagnosis and initial management			
BP2 – percentage of patients with hypertension whose notes record smoking status at least once	25	90	10
BP3 – percentage of patients with hypertension who smoke whose notes contain a record that smoking cessation advice has been offered at least once	25	90	10
Ongoing management			
BP4 – percentage of patients with hypertension for whom there is a record of blood pressure in the past 9 months	25	90	20
BP5 – percentage of patients with hypertension in whom the last blood pressure (in last 9 months) is 150/90 or less	25	70	56

patient experience (100 points). Clinical indicators are divided into 10 clinical areas (Table 6-3), of which the most heavily weighted are coronary heart disease (121 points), hypertension (105) and diabetes (99).

Table 6-4 illustrates how the scheme works for one clinical area – hypertension. Five indicators are used, covering structure (clinical records), process (diagnosis and initial management) and outcome. Most indicators have a lower limit (at which points start to be earned) and a maximum number of points. The points available for each indicator are shown in the right hand column. For example, points start to accumulate for indicator BP2 once the notes of 25% of patients with hypertension record their smoking status at least once. A maximum of 10 points is secured when the smoking status of 90% of patients is recorded.

The new GP contract is one of the most ambitious attempts to combine clinical-quality targets and incentives within physicians' remuneration (Smith and York 2004). It has some parallels with the performance-ratings regime. However, clinical quality plays a much greater role in the GP contract than in performance ratings. Also, individual earnings are much more directly at risk so much of the contract represents a step into the unknown. It embodies a number of important strengths, in line with the prescriptions of standard economic models. Most importantly, it seeks to reward cost-effective practice in the form of the structure, processes and outcome of health care. The scheme has been developed in close collaboration with physicians who have sought to apply evidence-based principles to the selection of performance indicators. Efforts have been made to ensure that the indicators are consistent with national clinical guidelines.

The structure of the scheme offers some important advances. Its balanced scorecard approach seeks to reflect the relative importance of different primary-care activities in terms of impact on health. By basing remuneration on an aggregate score, GPs remain free to decide their own priorities and thus may avoid many of the distortions associated with more piecemeal schemes. The scheme rewards practices (rather than individual physicians), so is likely to encourage teamwork and peer review. In contrast to many previous incentive schemes, the new contract can make a real difference to GP incomes. Finally, there is a commitment to review and update the incentive scheme.

Notwithstanding these apparent strengths, there are some potential risks. First, because it is a complex scheme, GPs may not understand its full implications and may not respond as intended. Second, important areas of activity not covered by the scheme may be downgraded. For example, mental health is allotted a mere 41 points, despite its importance in primary care. The contract documentation notes:

> …it was not possible to develop indicators that could be rewarded in this type of framework for many of the most important aspects of mental-health care. Mental-health care is however an example of a number of conditions where some markers of good clinical care have been included in the organizational indicators.

It will be important to evaluate whether this approach is adequate. It will also be important to check whether the scheme adversely affects some of the softer quality attributes of primary care that are not directly rewarded (such as continuity of care) or collaborative actions with other public services. The new contract may discourage clinical practice in challenging environments. GPs are contracted to accept all types on their lists and are not allowed to cream off healthy or compliant patients. In practice, GPs may find ways to discourage enrolment of patients who adversely affect performance measures. Perhaps even more importantly, the scheme may not do enough to encourage GPs to set up practice in disadvantaged areas. The initial implementation has sought to adjust performance measures for local environmental difficulties by weighting payments in the clinical domain according to measures of disease prevalence. It will be an important evaluation task to determine whether these adjustments have operated effectively and fairly.

There is also a risk of gaming and misrepresentation. Some of the performance measures appear to be particularly vulnerable in this respect. There is great potential for misrepresentation given that the scheme relies mostly on self-reported data. Even if fraud is rare, the scheme may be undermined if GPs perceive there to be widespread inaccuracy in reporting. A cost-effective audit regime is required, supported by a professional culture that does not tolerate misdemeanours. In the longer term, issues such as public release of performance data may need to be addressed.

Thus, although the design and implementation of the GP scheme is a major achievement in itself, it will require regular monitoring and review. About 90% of practices secured maximum points in the first year of implementation, far in excess of expectations. However, as no evaluation scheme has yet been published it is impossible to say whether this is because the targets are too easy or because GP performance has improved dramatically. The key tasks now are to answer these and other important questions; identify any unintended (and unwanted) consequences; incorporate new clinical evidence as it emerges; and refine the architecture of the scheme. This evaluation and monitoring may impose a substantial managerial burden. Traditionally, the NHS has reported very low managerial costs; the public and politicians are reluctant to recognize that management activity may make an important contribution to clinical quality. Nevertheless, investment in information, consultation and managerial processes is needed if the full benefits of the GP scheme are to be secured.

Finally, perhaps the most uncertain element of any incentive scheme is whether it might undermine the professional ethics and morale of physicians. The medical profession arose in part from a need to guide the actions of physicians in circumstances lacking direct guidance or remuneration. Will such a heavy reliance on explicit use of incentives make them less willing to respond in the best interests of patients when not directly rewarded? Frey (1997) hypothesizes that excessive reliance on external incentives may "drive out" internal motivation. If this is so, and the effectiveness of those professionals declines as a result, there may be considerable costs from such heavy reliance on external motivation.

Discussion

The experience with targets has developed very rapidly in the English health system over a period of 15 years. The first tentative steps (in public health) were largely ineffective and initial ambitions were modest when attention switched to health-service delivery. However, the introduction of a targets culture throughout English public services has rapidly increased the prominence and impact of targets in the NHS. The two most high-profile examples have been the performance ratings of NHS organizations and the quality incentives embodied in the GP contract.

There are a number of reasons for the increasing influence of targets in England.

• Their range and specificity has increased markedly moving from long-term, general objectives towards very precise, short-term targets. This has been accompanied by a proliferation of targets.

• The specification has progressed from national to organizational to practice level. This local interpretation of national targets is likely to have much more resonance with individual practitioners.

• There have been some attempts (at least with the GP contract) to engage professionals with the design and implementation of the targets' regime. Whilst running the risk of capture by professional interests, this also increases the chance that professionals will take notice of the targets.

• Organizations have been given increased capacity to respond to challenging targets, through extra finance, information and managerial expertise.

Finally, and perhaps most crucially, concrete incentives have been attached to the targets. The GP contract has only been made possible by a large injection of additional finance.

It is noteworthy that the recent English target initiatives have combined a multiplicity of targets into a single indicator of performance at the local level (performance rating for NHS organizations, quality scores for general practices). Providing that the method of aggregating individual indicators is in line with national objectives, these composite measures of success can play a particularly important role in allowing local organizations or practitioners to choose the areas of endeavour on which they wish to concentrate. The alternative of requiring improvement in every domain diminishes such local autonomy and may be less effective.

Without question, the use of a single indicator of success is a highly effective means of securing popular, political and media attention on performance issues and shaping public debate. Many commentators regret the crude simplification and value judgements needed to create such composite indicators. Yet, without this mechanism, it seems that important performance data will not secure the attention of managers, the public, patients or politicians (Mannion and Goddard 2001). Public provision of data is a necessary but not sufficient condition for heightened sensitivity to performance issues. It must be accompanied by imaginative presentational innovations, with the composite indicator appearing to be amongst the most effective (Smith 2002). England has taken the lead in pursuing this principle across the public services.

Some serious risks associated with the current English targets regime are noted.

- Targets are selective, and untargeted aspects of the health system may be neglected.

- If incentives are not designed carefully, managers and practitioners are likely to concentrate on short-term targets directly within their control at the expense of targets that address longer-term or less controllable objectives.

- The targets' system is very complex, requiring capacity to implement it and giving rise to the scope for capture by professional interests.

- Excessively aggressive targets may undermine the reliability of the data on which they depend.

- Excessively aggressive targets may induce gaming or other undesirable labour market responses as clinicians and managers seek to create favourable environments for achieving them.

- The targets regime may replace altruistic professional motivation with a narrow mercenary viewpoint.

To date, most of the evidence regarding such risks is anecdotal. A full evaluation of the costs and benefits of any English targets' system is still awaited. This is intrinsically difficult but should weigh carefully the costs associated with perverse outcomes against the manifest gains that have been secured. However, all of the risks can be mitigated to some extent by the introduction of countervailing instruments where necessary.

The discussion suggests a need for a powerful national-level regulator to monitor the operation of the targets; assure the reliability of data; and keep the targets' regime updated. In order to retain trust at all levels, this regulator must be seen to be clearly independent of all interest groups such as government, providers, professionals and patient groups. At the local level, organizations must have the capacity to understand and act on the messages embodied in the targets' regime. The English experiments are at an early stage, and have induced some unintended and undesired outcomes. However, they do seem to be effecting a real change in health-system behaviour to a much greater extent than previous instruments. The future challenges are to undertake careful monitoring; nurture the benefits of targets; and neutralize their harmful side-effects.

REFERENCES

Adshead F, Thorpe A (2005). Delivering "Choosing Health".*Public Health,* 119:954-957.

Barker R, Pearce M, Irving M (2004). Star wars, NHS style. *BMJ,* 329:107-109.

Bevan G, Hood C (2006). Have targets improved performance in the English NHS? *British Medical Journal,* 332:419-422.

Department of Health (1991). *The Patient's Charter.* London, Department of Health.

Department of Health (1992). *The Health of the Nation.* London, HMSO.

Department of Health (1998). *Health of the Nation: a policy assessed.* London, Department of Health.

Department of Health (2000). *The NHS Plan: a plan for investment, a plan for reform.* London, The Stationery Office.

Department of Health (2001) NHS performance ratings. Acute Trusts 2000/01 (http://www.dh.gov.uk/en/Publicationsandstatistics/Publications/PublicationsPolicyAndGuidance/DH_4002706, accessed 19 May 2008).

Department of Health (2003). *Investing in general practice: the new GMS contract.* London, Department of Health.

Department of Health (2004). *Choosing health: making healthy choices easier.* London, Department of Health.

Frey B (1997). A constitution for knaves crowds out civic virtues. *Economic Journal,* 107(443):1043-1053.

Hauck K, Rice N, Smith P (2003). The influence of health care organizations on indicators of health system performance. *Journal of Health Services Research and Policy,* 8(2):68-74.

Hauck K, Street A (2004). *Do targets matter? A comparison of English and Welsh national health priorities.* York, Centre for Health Economics, University of York.

Healthcare Commission [web site]. London, Healthcare Commission. (http://ratings2004.healthcarecommission.org.uk/home.asp, accessed 26 April 2005).

Healthcare Commission (2004). *Performance ratings 2003/2004.* London, Healthcare Commission.

Healthcare Commission (2005). *Assessment for improvement. The annual health check. Measuring what matters.* London, Healthcare Commission.

HM Treasury (1999). *Public services for the future: modernisation, reform, accountability.* London, The Stationery Office.

HM Treasury (2004). *Stability, security and opportunity for all: investing for Britain's long term future. Public spending plans 2005-2008.* London, HM Treasury.

Hood C, Bevan G (2005). *Governance by targets and terror: synecdoche, gaming and audit.* Oxford, All Souls College.

House of Commons Public Administration Select Committee (2003). *On target? Government by measurement. Fifth Report of Session 2002-03.* London, The Stationery Office.

Hunter D (2002). England. In: Marinker M, eds. *Health targets in Europe.* London, BMJ Books.

Klein R (1995). *The new politics of the NHS.* London, Longman.

Le Grand J, Mays N, Mulligan J, eds. (1998). *Learning from the NHS internal market.* London, King's Fund Institute.

Mannion R, Davies H, Marshall M (2005). Impact of star performance ratings in English acute hospital trusts. *Journal of Health Services Research and Policy,* 10(1):18-24.

Mannion R, Goddard M (2001). Impact of published clinical outcomes data: case study in NHS hospital trusts. *BMJ,* 323:260-263.

Marks L, Hunter D (2005). Moving upstream or muddying the waters? Incentives for managing for health. *Public Health,* 119:974-980.

Martin S, Smith PC (1999). Rationing by waiting lists: an empirical investigation. *Journal of Public Economics,* 71(1):141-164.

Nove A (1980). *The Soviet economic system, 2nd edition.* London, Allen and Unwin.

Smith P (1995). On the unintended consequences of publishing performance data in the public sector. *International Journal of Public Administration,* 18(2/3): 277-310.

Smith P (2002). Developing composite indicators for assessing overall system efficiency. In: Smith P, ed. *Measuring up: improving health systems performance in OECD countries.* Paris, Organisation for Economic Co-operation and Development.

Smith P, Goddard M (2000). Reforming health care markets. In: Smith P, ed. *Reforming markets in health care: an economic perspective.* Buckingham, Open University Press.

Smith P, York N (2004). Quality incentives: the case of UK general practitioners. *Health Affairs,* 23(3):112-118.

Wanless D (2002). *Securing our future health: taking a long-term view.* London, HM Treasury.

Chapter 7

Flanders: Health Targets as a Catalyst for Action

Stephan Van den Broucke

Introduction

Constitutionally, Belgium is a federal state incorporating three language-based communities (Dutch-, French- and German-speaking) since 1993. According to the constitution, these communities have political autonomy in areas that are "person-related", which includes preventive health care. In the Flemish (i.e. Dutch-speaking) community, this autonomy has resulted in (among other things) the creation of a legal and organizational framework for preventive health care and health promotion. The development of a long-term policy vision entailed the formulation of a series of health targets (in 1997 and 2002) outlining the priorities for preventive health and health promotion and specifying the desired outcomes of policies and actions.

This chapter begins by providing a critical analysis of the development and implementation of the Flemish health targets, looking at the key actors in this process as well as the anticipated role and aims of the targets, their contents and formulation. Subsequent sections address the instruments and means to implement them; the use of intelligence in their definition and monitoring; and any unintended and undesirable outcomes.

Historical overview

Before political devolution in the 1980 and 1990s, preventive health care in Belgium received relatively little attention from policy-makers. Despite widespread agreement with the principle that prevention is better than cure, policy initiatives and resulting expenditure focused strongly on curative services. Most preventive measures entailed subsidizing a limited number of structured government-organized services in primary health care and secondary prevention such as mother and child care; school medical services; occupational health; and tuberculosis and cancer screening. On the other hand, primary prevention and health education were left to nongovernmental organizations. These organizations could be supported by government subsidies but were largely dependent on lobbying, media attention and the personal interests of politicians. This resulted in a lack of continuity and no sustained policy based on empirical evidence or a long-term strategy.

This situation changed dramatically at the beginning of the 1990s against the background of rising costs for health care. There was growing awareness that a continued investment limited to curative services would make health care unaffordable. Prevention received a new mandate, inspired by WHO's Health for All programme (WHO Regional Office for Europe 1999 ; WHO Regional Office for Europe 1985). This renewed attention to prevention was boosted by the new political situation in 1993 in which the language-based communities were given more autonomy. In the Flemish community, consecutive ministers in charge of health used this momentum to reorient preventive health policy drastically, changing the focus of activities as well as the structures and policy-making processes.

Within the focus of activities, the concept of prevention was widened to include health promotion. In addition to the more established medical prevention programmes, new initiatives enhanced people's control of the determinants of their health by empowering individuals, groups and communities to change their lifestyles and/or through decision-makers' actions to change the conditions which affect health. Within the structure, established preventive services were complemented by organizations within and outside the health sector to create possibilities for intra- and intersectoral collaboration. In addition, the establishment of local health networks (LHNs) made the local community the pre-eminent level for preventive actions. These were charged with the coordination of local actors involved in preventive health care as well as the planning, implementation and evaluation of local prevention projects. Finally, for policy processes, it was decided to adopt a health target based approach to coordinate the actions of all organizations working in preventive health.

This approach was inspired by the examples of other countries and subnational entities that had used health targets, in particular the United States of America, Australia, New Zealand, England, Scotland, Wales, Canada and the Netherlands (Nutbeam and Wise 1996). It also fitted with the broader Flemish policy context, strongly inspired by the principles of management by objectives and evidence based policy-making. This was exemplified by the drafting of an overall strategic plan for Flanders in the mid 1990s and by the use of regional indicators in all policy sectors for which the Flemish Government is responsible (Vanweddingen 2004).

The first Flemish health targets were introduced in January 1998, following government agreement on five health targets to be achieved in the period from 1998 to 2002. These targets were concerned with smoking, nutrition, breast cancer screening, injury prevention and vaccine coverage. They followed the recommendation of the Flemish Health Council, the official advisory body to the Flemish Government and Parliament on health-related issues. This drew heavily on the Health for All targets established by the WHO European Region (WHO Regional Office for Europe 1985) and on an analysis of the main health threats as reflected in the available mortality and morbidity statistics for Flanders (Aelvoet et al. 1997).

These first Flemish health targets were generally welcomed by both politicians and practitioners as an improvement on existing health policy (Beck undated). They also met some criticism on their content, in particular the health topics to which they referred. Some opponents considered that the targets focused too much on health-related behaviours (e.g. smoking, nutrition, prevention of injuries) and not enough on medical conditions and health status. Others felt that the targets were too selective, failing to address all the lifestyle factors listed in the Health for All documents and omitting important behaviours such as alcohol abuse, drug use, unsafe sexual practices or violence. It was also said that the targets did not pay attention to mental health or health inequalities. Furthermore, the targets were considered too nonspecific from a methodological point of view – the lack of baseline measures would make evaluation problematic.

Despite these concerns, the health targets were accepted by the Flemish Parliament as a basis for action during the period from 1998 to 2002. Their role was re-emphasized by the Flemish Minister of Health who took office after the 1999 elections. Proposals to make the targets more specific were not implemented and the originals continued to be used, even after the end of the first five-year term in 2002. An additional target, focusing on the prevention of depression and suicide, was formulated in 2002 to cover the period until 2010. This sixth health target was endorsed by the Flemish government[6] in 2006 and was followed by an action plan for suicide prevention launched in 2007, serving as a basis to allocate funds to relevant projects and campaigns. In 2008 a new target on nutrition and physical activity is foreseen.

---

[6] The Flemish health target on the prevention of depression and suicide was launched in 2004 and discussed in the Parliamentary Commission on Health but not in Parliament. It was endorsed by the Flemish government in 2006 after the executive decision to bring a new decree on the reorganization of the preventive health sector into effect.

All six of the health targets were reaffirmed following the 2004 elections and subsequent inauguration of a new Flemish government. However, modifications to broaden the scope of certain targets were envisaged. Specifically, the target on tobacco prevention will probably be expanded to include substance abuse more generally. The target on nutrition will incorporate enhanced physical activity and will also refer explicitly to obesity.

These expected changes notwithstanding, the health targets continue to serve as a point of reference for Flemish preventive health policy. Continued political support for the targets can be inferred from the fact that policy documents refer explicitly to them (Community of Flanders 2004; Vlaams Minister van Welzijn and Volksgezondheid en Gezin 2004) and that progress towards attaining the targets is the subject of questions in the Flemish Parliament (Vlaams Parlement 2005). While the principle of working with health targets seems well-accepted, there is an overall feeling that the targets themselves should be evaluated and fine-tuned – their use as a policy tool can be enhanced by developing better indicators to monitor progress and collaborative actions to achieve them. These issues have been proposed as the next steps, to be incorporated in forthcoming legislature. A key issue is how to increase collaboration at the federal (Belgian) policy level. As many key policies are taken at this level the Flemish health targets could act as a lever for further discussion on health policy throughout Belgium.

Implementation of the Flemish health targets

The introduction of the Flemish health targets raised high expectations, based on the experience of other countries that had adopted a target-based approach. It was expected that target setting would enable more effective management of preventive health policies; raise the visibility of prevention; enhance collaboration between relevant organizations; contribute to the overall quality and effectiveness of preventive interventions; and ultimately improve the health status of the population. Furthermore, it was believed that the introduction of targets would lead to the development of better indicators to monitor changes in population health status (Van den Broucke and Denekens 1999).

A number of initiatives were undertaken in order to fulfil these expectations. The majority were performed by the Flemish Ministry of Health, the main driving force behind the target-based approach. Probably the most important initiative was the drafting of a new law on prevention in 2003. The decree regarding preventive health care[7] specifically referred to the principle of working with health targets; outlined the procedures to update or formulate new targets; and identified the different partners that could contribute towards their achievement. Partners involved include the Flemish Institute for Health Promotion, the Flemish League Against Cancer and centres for mental health. Their contributions are set out in mutual agreements or covenants that specify the actions to be undertaken within a given time in return for public funding, and performance indicators to evaluate the organizations' achievements. In effect, the Ministry can delegate specific tasks to these organizations while retaining control of overall policy direction. The Ministry of Health hired additional staff to strengthen the capacity to initiate policies on prevention and health promotion and to evaluate the performance of the expert organizations involved. The Ministry of Health also gained more authority as a result.

The establishment of LHNs in 1998 was particularly important. These partnerships between preventive health organizations working at the local level serve between 250 000 and 400 000 inhabitants. With the main task of stimulating collaboration between organizations involved in prevention they collect information on existing activities; support joint planning; and evaluate primary prevention and health promotion projects. Each LHN has a multidisciplinary staff of 2.5 full-time equivalents at their disposal (1 full-time coordinator, 1 staff member and 1 part-time administrative assistant). They are supported financially by the Flemish Government under covenants that specify the actions to be performed during three-year periods, most of which arise from the Flemish health targets. The entire area of Flanders has been covered by 26 LHNs since 2000.

These measures had a profound impact on the organization of preventive health care in Flanders but did not achieve all of the expected effects. The introduction of the health targets did not produce a fundamental change in the focus of preventive health policy as it did not strengthen the emphasis on activities concerning the achievement of the targets or the reallocation of resources. The targets neither increased the effectiveness of preventive interventions nor produced the desired health gains. For example, the percentage of smokers actually increased slightly between 1998 and 2002, mainly as a result of higher smoking initiation among young females. While the percentage of male smokers dropped (35.5% to 32.8%), the percentage of female smokers increased (22% to 22.8%). That of female smokers aged 15-24 increased from 20.8% to 27.3% (Cloots et al. 2002). Similarly,

---

[7] Under Belgian constitutional law, a decree is a law issued by a regional government. This distinguishes it from a law issued by the federal Belgian government.

although the diet of Flemish citizens contained less fat in 2001 than in 1997, young people's diets actually became less healthy. The number of fatal home injuries dropped by 5% between 1998 and 2001 but the number of fatal traffic accidents did not fall markedly. Only a slight increase in immunization rates was achieved. In fact, the breast cancer screening target was the only one that was fully achieved: by 2002, an intensive campaign organized by the Flemish government led to an 80% increase in the number of women in the 50-69 year target group who participated in screening.

To some extent, this failure to reach the targets may be because the expected changes require more time. On the other hand, it is also clear that a number of conditions necessary for a successful implementation of the health targets were not fulfilled. First, implementation plans were elaborated belatedly although it is generally recommended that health targets are accompanied by strategies which specify the ways in which they can be achieved (van Herten and Gunning-Schepers 2000). For the targets on tobacco prevention, nutrition and injury prevention, the strategies to specify intermediate targets were developed only in 2004, well after the end of the initial five-year period in which they should have been achieved (Flemish Institute for Health Promotion 2004; Flemish Platform for Accident Prevention 2004; Flemish Platform for Tobacco Prevention 2004). No explicit strategies and only isolated projects were developed for the targets on breast cancer screening, vaccination and depression and suicide.

Second, political responsibility for achieving the targets has remained unclear. The Flemish health targets were endorsed by the Flemish Parliament and integrated into the overall policy of the Flemish Government. Although the Flemish Minister of Health was made accountable for their achievement, in reality responsibility for failure to achieve the targets resides with the organizations charged with their implementation. Moreover, it is not clear whether there are any consequences for failing to reach the targets; no measures resulted from the failure to hit the first five targets by 2002.

Third, there is no clear ownership of the health targets. Their narrow individual focus prevented their adoption as shared priorities by all those engaged in prevention. Thus, although the targets were meant to guide the actions of all organizations involved in preventive health care, responsibility for achieving them is left largely to a small number. Apart from the LHNs, these include the Flemish Institute for Health Promotion, which develops methods relevant to the targets that involve health promotion (tobacco control, nutrition, injury prevention); and a number of mental health organizations. Most of these organizations are very small, lack human and organizational capacity; and, given the novelty of the tasks to be undertaken, have a limited professionally trained workforce.

Finally, the targets outlined the priorities for prevention during the 1997-2002 period and onwards to 2010. However, only part of the budget necessary to achieve these priorities was allocated. No additional resources were made available for targets on smoking, nutrition and injury prevention. The overall budget for health promotion has remained virtually unchanged (€ 6.4 million in 1997, € 7 million in 2004) – roughly € 1.25 per inhabitant (Van den Broucke and Stevens 2001). Moreover, a large share of this budget is allocated to existing structures such as the Flemish Institute for Health Promotion (approximately € 1.2 million per year), or to topics outside the health targets, particularly HIV/AIDS prevention (€ 2.28 million per year). The situation is more encouraging for targets related to medical interventions – with additional financial resources budgeted for breast cancer screening (€ 4 644 000 in 2004) and immunization against infectious diseases (€ 6 068 000 in 2004). A small budget is reserved for specific projects and campaigns for the prevention of depression and suicide (€ 372 000 in 2002; € 439 000 in 2003). Finally, some resources are provided to fund LHN operations (€ 973 000 in 2004).

Yet the implementation of the health targets did have some effects. Their introduction and the drafting of the preventive health decree generated a great deal of political interest in prevention and health promotion, and were the subject of political debate at both Flemish and the local level. Moreover, the introduction of covenants facilitated the implementation of prevention by providing the Ministry of Health with an instrument to monitor the activities of key organizations and to focus attention on the health targets. This helps to avoid overlapping projects or contradictory messages arising from the fragmentation of health-promotion activities. At the same time, the covenant system reduces the autonomy of these organizations and leads to a more top-down approach in prevention policy. On a structural level, the establishment of the LHNs encourages the exchange of information between local organizations and creates possibilities for collaboration by offering a focal point for preventive actions. One recent study demonstrated that participating organizations perceive the LHNs to be useful, creating greater synergy in their efforts to address common objectives, including the pursuit of health targets. Finally, the introduction of the health targets also broadened the scope of prevention. Through the LHNs, established organizations for preventive health care are encouraged to collaborate with other sectors such as education and welfare, and with local government. This multisectoral and interdisciplinary approach on a local level is exemplified in the actions outlined in Box 7-1 and Box 7-2.

In summary, although health target setting in Flanders has not yet produced the expected health gains, it has introduced a number of changes in the policy process and, even more notably, in the organization of prevention. These changes may set the stage for more effective actions in coming years.

Defining the Flemish health targets

The Flemish Government's decision to use a target-based approach for preventive health reflected its aspiration to introduce a proactive and efficient style of governance, as well as a belief that facts and figures provide a better basis for policy development than political intuition. These ambitions were complemented by a broad view on health. This is exemplified by the fact that, in accordance with WHO recommendations (WHO Regional Office for

Box 7-1 *Both feet on the ground: a programme to prevent falls among senior citizens in Brussels*

This programme was developed by the Brussels' LHN to reduce the number of accidental falls among senior citizens. It is important for the well-being of senior citizens that they stay independent within their own environments but those who live alone have a high risk of falling. Apart from the (often very serious) physical consequences, falls can also have a huge impact on mental health. The fear of falling again may reduce confidence, decrease mobility and/or increase loneliness.

The programme involves a number of activities to reduce the risk of falling among senior citizens. A series of local actions not only aim to raise awareness about the risks of falling but also pay attention to structural measures that make houses safer. The LHN relies on the input of various partners represented in the network in order to carry out these activities:

• educational activities on preventing falls, use of medication, osteoporosis
• training health and social workers about these issues
• advice on structural adaptations to houses
• GPs or physical therapists identify people or groups at risk
• promotion of physical activity
• articles in the local press
• information packages

The programme started as a pilot project in one district (Brussels West) in 1999-2001, and was implemented more broadly in several other districts (Anderlecht, Sint-Jans-Molenbeek, Ukkel, Vorst) between 2002 and 2004.

Box 7-2 *School fruit: enhancing healthy nutrition in Leuven schools*

The school fruit project started in 2000, when two primary schools in Leuven collaborated with a local fruit market to provide their pupils with a healthy snack – a piece of fruit each week. By 2004 it had grown into an action programme involving 20 000 pupils at 60 schools in 13 communities around Leuven. More than 600 000 pieces of fruit have been distributed and 10 different fruit producers and retailers participate in the project.

• The project relies on collaboration between different local actors for health.
• Government of the local community puts the issue on the school council agenda, seeks potential suppliers, coordinates orders and evaluates the project.
• Teachers and principals bring the project to the attention of parents, evaluate the extra workload and secure its continuity.
• Parent committees in schools take the lead by offering practical support for the distribution of fruit, drawing attention to the project during school activities and seeking additional funding.
• Children and parents participate in the project and look for additional activities.
• The LHN team coordinates activities and takes charge of the communication between stakeholders and external partners.

Several local governments (communes) provide logistic and/or financial support for the project to ensure that practical demands on the schools can be kept to a minimum. In addition, the LHN provides educational materials and background information on healthy nutrition. The project is sustainable because of the low cost of the action – € 5-10 per child per year.

Box 7-3 *Selected General health targets from Flanders*

• 10% reduction in the number of smokers among women and men, especially among young people;
• significant reduction in the consumption of fat in food, leading to diets with low fat and highi fibre;
• more effective breast cancer screening – 80% increase in the number of screenings in the target group of women aged 50-69, reaching 75% of the women in the target group;
• 20% reduction in the number of fatal injuries at home and on the roads;
• significant improvement in the prevention of infectious diseases by increasing vaccine coverage for polio, whooping cough, diphtheria, tetanus, measles, mumps and rubella;
• 8% reduction in the number of deaths due to suicide among men and women compared with the year 2000.

Europe 1999; WHO Regional Office for Europe 1985), the health targets address the main determinants of health in industrialized countries rather than focusing on specific conditions or diseases. In addition, the inclusion of the mental-health target reflects a holistic view of health. Rather than merely paying lip service to these principles, the Flemish health targets show ambition to bring about actual change in the areas of interest. Some of these targets are presented in Box 7-3.

If targets are to be achieved, it is essential that the organizations concerned accept them to be legitimate, relevant and feasible. This implies involvement in the process to define targets. Partner organizations had limited participation in the first five Flemish targets. Their formulation was essentially expert driven, following proposals from the Flemish Health Council. In turn, they drew extensively on the Health for All targets for the WHO European Region (WHO 1985 1999) and on the analysis of the burden of disease in Flanders (Aelvoet et al. 1997; Ministerie van de Vlaamse Gemeenschap 1997). The potential years of life lost were a major factor in setting priorities. Rather than applying a formal method such as extrapolation or benchmarking to arrive at the target formulation from these data, the available statistics were used pragmatically. This explains the methodological criticism of the targets, which were considered too nonspecific and not sufficiently evidence based. For example, "young people" is not defined in the target to reduce the number of smokers among young people. Similarly, the target on healthy nutrition does not specify what would be a "significant" reduction. Finally, the lack of a baseline measure for some of the targets is a serious shortcoming.

Epidemiological data provided important inputs to target definitions but they were not the only consideration. Target formulation also drew on a strategic health promotion plan drafted by the Flemish Institute for Health Promotion (Lievens and Van Den Broucke 1995) while considering what was actually attainable, given existing knowledge and organizational capacity in the sector. However, there was no systematic assessment of the sector's capacity. Consistent with the emphasis on consensus (Brown and Redman 1995), health targets should also reflect broader societal concerns as well as the viewpoint of the organizations involved in their implementation.

Formulation of the last target (on prevention of depression and suicide) addressed these shortcomings by using a different approach. In an effort to achieve wide participation, a health conference was organized by working groups of experts coordinated by the Flemish Ministry of Health. These were intended to secure a sufficient evidence base for the target definition by relying on epidemiological data and evidence of good practice. This approach aimed to attain a balance between a technocratic approach (emphasizing epidemiology and the scope for intervention) and a participatory approach (emphasizing democratic legitimacy, participation and alliance building) (van Herten and Gunning-Schepers 2000). In reality the approach remained strongly expert-driven, the input of practitioners was minimal or symbolic and therefore the target's degree of ownership remained low. Nevertheless, the decree on preventive health care identified the organization of a health conference as the method of choice to define or review health targets. Towards the end of 2008 a new health conference will be organized to formulate a new health target on nutrition and physical activity.

Exerting influence

To ensure that health targets are being implemented, it is necessary for policy-makers to be able to influence the various actors and processes that may contribute. The Flemish Ministry of Health was the driving force behind the definition of health targets and applied a variety of mechanisms to exert influence on organizations within the preventive health sector.

Some of these mechanisms may be considered directive or top-down because they coerce organizations to take particular actions. One example is the regulatory framework created via the preventive health decree which provides a legal basis for synchronizing their activities. In a similar vein, the system of covenants provides the Ministry of Health with a legal instrument not only to direct organizations to pay more attention to the health targets but also to evaluate their performance.

Less direct measures were also taken to exert influence on the actors and processes in the health sector. For instance, the creation of the LHNs promoted collaboration between key organizations involved in health care at the local level and resulted in more synergetic efforts to achieve the targets. Similarly, budgets (however limited) allocated for projects that aimed to realize the targets provided incentives for organizations. This project-based approach introduces an element of competition between actors and offers the Ministry of Health more flexibility and control over their initiatives. An additional advantage is that by investing in well-defined activities, the government can rightfully claim to "fund actions instead of structures". On the other hand, project-based actions can become isolated if they are not integrated within a broader strategy.

In contrast, few measures were taken to influence actors or processes outside the health sector. Flemish health targets were endorsed by the Flemish Parliament, therefore (theoretically) owned by the entire Flemish Government, but no efforts were made to include health targets in non-health sector policies. For example, no explicit link was made to integrate the health targets in goals for primary and secondary education developed by the Ministry of Education. As a result, despite their formal role in prevention and health promotion, school counselling centres are not systematically involved in efforts to achieve these targets. Similarly, the Ministry of Environment and Infrastructure elaborated the strategic plan for traffic and mobility that addresses road safety without referring to the health target on injury prevention. These are missed important opportunities to build partnerships with key actors in other sectors and develop intersectoral approaches.

Collecting and using intelligence

One of the Flemish Government's main reasons for introducing health targets was its ambition to establish an evidence-based preventive health policy. An important consideration is what counts as evidence and how it can be assessed. Scientific, professional and community groups make legitimate claims to have relevant expertise but their views often compete (Rada et al. 1999). In general, evidence deriving from empirical research (e.g. randomized control trials or cohort studies) is regarded as the most reliable form of evidence. Expert opinions (either individual or a consensus) occupy the lowest level in the evidence hierarchy and may not be considered useful or appropriate for decision-making (Aro et al. 2005). Nevertheless, expert opinions can be used to interpret research evidence (Rychetnik et al. 2004) and experts can function as information sources.

Both kinds of evidence were used to define the Flemish health targets. As explained earlier, the first five health targets were not only based on the analysis of the burden of disease derived from mortality and morbidity statistics, but also drew on expert opinions to assess their relevance and attainability – as in the strategic plan for health promotion (Lievens & Van den Broucke 1995). Likewise, the working groups preparing the health conference on depression and suicide drew on epidemiological data from Flanders and neighbouring countries, as well as evidence of cost-effective interventions. The latter was used to select a limited number of preventive interventions to be funded as pilot projects.

Reliance on published research to select prevention strategies can introduce a bias in favour of interventions that lend themselves to empirical study. More complex interventions, such as community-based programmes that combine mutually reinforcing methods and actions, are studied less often. Similarly, there are very few published studies on the effects of interventions that aim to influence the more distal determinants of health (especially mental health);

have no simple relationship with specific health conditions; and often interact with other risk or protective factors. This bias influenced the prevention of depression health target – the chosen intervention strategies were aimed predominantly at early detection and secondary prevention, rather than promoting mental health by addressing its broader determinants. Also, hardly any of the chosen interventions involved participation from other sectors.

A similar bias towards the use of available evidence can be seen in monitoring the achievement of health targets. This used existing indicators, including the Flemish mortality and morbidity data (Cloots et al. 2002); records from a sentinel network of GPs (Van Casteren and Leurquin 1992); and empirical data on health-related behaviour derived from population-based surveys such as the Belgian Health Interview Survey (HIS) (Demarest 2001; Demarest et al. 2005) and the study on Health Behaviour in School-aged Children (HBSC) (Vereecken et al. 1998). The HIS measures perceived health, health-service utilization and health-related behaviour in a representative sample of the Belgian population at four-yearly intervals. The HBSC is part of an international study by a consortium sponsored by WHO (Currie et al. 2004). It involves the assessment of health-related behaviours, lifestyle factors and well-being in a representative sample of children (11-18 years) every two or four years.

These sources provide important information about population health status and the behavioural factors related to health. Allowing detection of changes over time, they are useful for monitoring progress towards targets but are not linked to specific interventions. Moreover, the available indicators are mostly aggregated at national or regional levels and cannot be broken down to local level where the actions to achieve targets occur. Finally, the existing indicators are concerned with the outcomes of actions and programmes and do not pay attention to the inputs (e.g. budget, staffing, number of services or programmes, quality of implementation, etc.) or throughputs (i.e. processes linking inputs and outputs, such as participation rates, levels of acceptance by participants, perceived quality of interventions, collaboration between organizations, intermediate outcomes). Without information about these, it is impossible to monitor the processes involved in achieving health targets, assess the contribution of different interventions and decide which strategies to pursue or to alter.

In an effort to collect information on these aspects, the Flemish Institute for Health Promotion developed a computerized system to monitor LHN activities (Scheerder and Van den Broucke 2001), based on Nutbeam's outcome model for health promotion. Unfortunately, this system was never implemented. However, a series of indicators was developed for the implementation of smoking and nutrition policies in schools and workplaces (Flemish Institute for Health Promotion undated). In 2004, their application to 2742 Flemish schools and companies yielded important information about the achievement of this intermediate goal.

Lessons learned

The introduction of a target-based approach to preventive health care in Flanders was embedded within a broader reorientation. It coincided with the partial devolution of health policy and was strongly inspired by the principles of management by objectives and evidence-based policy-making, and by examples from other countries. Nearly ten years after their introduction, it is clear that health targets have become well-established as a health-policy tool. While their introduction has not yet produced the anticipated effects in terms of health gains or changes in the health-related behaviours on which they are focused, they have spurred a number of changes in the policy process. A number of lessons can be learned from this experience of using a target-based approach.

Firstly, the procedure to define health targets must anticipate their implementation. In order for targets to be achieved it is essential that ownership is created. They should not be forced upon the organizations that will deliver them and must be accepted as legitimate, relevant and feasible. Moreover, health targets should also reflect broad societal concerns. This requires the various stakeholders to be involved in the definition process. But targets should also be evidence based, maintaining a balance between participation and technical input using epidemiological data and/or expert opinions. There is potential in the health-conference approach used to involve experts and stakeholders in the definition of the target on depression and suicide prevention, but such participation must be genuine and not merely symbolic.

Secondly, a well-elaborated plan is required for successful implementation. Health targets should be accompanied by carefully selected strategies which specify the ways in which they can be achieved, at national (or regional) and local levels. These strategies should include intermediate targets, a realistic time frame and specify the actors that will be involved in their implementation. These can serve as reference points to select actions and as milestones for monitoring and evaluating the implementation process.

Other conditions for successful implementation of targets include securing sufficient financial means and human and organizational capacity. There is a need for a professional and well-trained workforce and an organizational structure with sufficient capacity to apply state-of-the-art knowledge and take action to achieve the targets. It also requires that actors in the field of prevention assume different professional roles. This entails more communication with other disciplines, some of which are relative newcomers to health concerns. This may require a reorientation of the training of health professionals, with more emphasis on methods for behaviour change and on multisectoral and multidisciplinary collaboration. Targets are unlikely to be achieved unless these conditions are fulfilled. It is the task of government to create these necessary preconditions.

Responsibility for achieving the targets should be clarified. Flemish health targets are endorsed by parliament and integrated in overall government policy, therefore ultimate responsibility for their achievement should lie with the policy-makers. It should not be shifted to the organizations charged with implementation. Moreover, the consequences of success or failure should be clarified. If the conditions necessary to implement the targets successfully have been fulfilled, failure to achieve them does not imply bad policy-making. Rather it is a call to redirect the strategies to achieve the targets. Such an approach would contribute to optimal use of health targets as a tool for policy-making and evaluation.

The Ministry of Health holds political responsibility for creating the conditions to achieve the targets while health-sector organizations are responsible for the actions to achieve them. However, health is influenced by a multitude of factors, many of which are outside the health sector. As these actors or processes have a key role in the achievement of the targets there should be efforts to include health targets in the policies of other sectors.

Participation by the organizations involved in prevention is a key factor for successful implementation of the health targets. Health ministries could achieve this by making more use of bottom-up mechanisms to encourage organizations to collaborate rather than applying only top-down mechanisms (e.g. creation of a regulatory framework, performance management via the covenant system). Such facilitating mechanisms could include allocating extra budgets for actions aimed at the targets; strengthening organizational and human capacity in public health; and enhancing the synergy between partners at regional and local level by encouraging collaborative implementation plans. Good stewardship uses facilitation rather than coercion alone.

Indicators that focus on mortality, morbidity and lifestyle are not sensitive enough to detect changes in intermediate outcomes (e.g. increased health literacy, introduction of non-smoking or health-nutrition policies in schools or workplaces) or changes in the conditions required to produce effects (e.g. policy changes, number and quality of actions undertaken to achieve health targets, participation rates, capacity, collaboration and synergy between organizations, etc.). Information about these elements is necessary to monitor the processes involved in achieving health targets; evaluate the contribution of different interventions; and decide which strategies to pursue or alter. In other words, a monitoring system should be put in place to cover the full range of inputs, throughputs and outputs related to the attainment of the health targets. Ideally, this should allow for the possibility of collecting information at a local (community) level, where many of the necessary actions take place. Furthermore, this monitoring system should include indicators that pay attention to quality of life in order to avoid a limited focus on disease.

By adopting a target-based approach, Flanders introduced a methodology to make preventive health-care policy and practice more evidence-based and goal-directed. It also moved away from a predominantly medically oriented policy towards a more holistic approach to preventive health. This is more in tune with the current needs of the post-modern society, paying attention to collaboration between different actors and sectors which impact on health. As in other countries that have adopted this approach, the experience in Flanders shows that the use of health targets can lead to a more transparent policy for prevention, enable better health policy processes and create more synergy among organizations in the field of prevention, health promotion and beyond. If the issues identified during the first ten years can be addressed, the value of health targets can be strengthened significantly and lead to more effective health policy in Flanders.

REFERENCES

Aelvoet W, Capet F, Vanoverloop J (1997). *Gezondheidsindicatoren 1996 (Health indicators 1996)*. Brussels, Ministerie van de Vlaamse Gemeenschap, Administratie Gezondheidszorg [Ministry of the Flemish Community, Administration for Health].

Aro AA, Van den Broucke S, Raty S (2005). Toward European consensus tools for reviewing the evidence and enhancing the quality of health promotion practice. *Promot Educ*, 21 (Suppl 1):10-14, 45-46, 55-56 passim.

Beck M (undated). *Ontwikkelling van doelstellingen en indicatoren omtrent preventief gezondheids-gerelateerd gedrag: Literatuurstudie en aanzet tot methodiekontwikkeling [Development of targets and indicators for preventive health related behaviour: literature study and development of methodology]*. Brussels, Vrije Universiteit Brussel [Free University of Brussels].

Brown WJ, Redman S (1995). Setting targets: a three-stage model for determining priorities for health promotion. *Aust J Public Health*, 19(3):263-269.

Cloots H, Hooft P, Smets H (2002). *Gezondheidsindicatoren 2001-2002 [Health indicators 2001-2002]*. Brussels, Ministerie van de Vlaamse Gemeenschap, Administratie Gezondheidszorg (Ministry of the Flemish Community, Administration for Health).

Community of Flanders (2004). Decreet betreffende het preventieve gezondheidsbeleid [Decree Regarding Preventive Health Care]. *Belgisch Staatsblad*, 03/02/2004: 6308-6321.

Currie C et al., eds. (2004). *Young people's health in context: international report from the HBSC 2001/02 survey.* Copenhagen, WHO Regional Office for Europe (WHO Policy Series: Health policy for children and adolescents, Issue 4).

Demarest S (2001). Health interview survey. *Archives of Public Health,* (5/6):219-221.

Demarest S et al. (2005). *Gezondheidsenquête door middel van Interview, België, 2001 [Health interview survey, Belgium, 2001].* Brussels, Scientific Institute of Public Health, Department of Epidemiology.

Flemish Institute for Health Promotion (2004). *Plan van aanpak ter bevordering van evenwichtig eten en regelmatige beweging: Aanbevelingen op Vlaams, regionaal en lokaal niveau [Implementation plan to promote a balanced diet and physical activity: recommendations on the Flemish, regional and local level].* Brussels, Flemish Institute for Health Promotion, Expert Group on Nutrition and Health.

Flemish Institute for Health Promotion (undated). *Voedings- en rookbeleid in scholen en bedrijven in kaart gebracht [Nutrition and smoking policies charted].* Brussels, Flemish Institute for Health Promotion.

Flemish Platform for Accident Prevention (2004). *Plan van aanpak voor Ongevallen in de privé-sfeer [Implementation plan to prevent accidents at home].* Brussels, Flemish Platform for Accident Prevention.

Flemish Platform for Tobacco Prevention (2004). *Plan van aanpak om het tabaksgebruik in Vlaanderen te verminderen [Implementation plan to reduce the use of tobacco in Flanders].* Brussels, Flemish Platform for Tobacco Prevention.

Lievens P, Van Den Broucke S (1995). Strategic planning for health promotion in a decentralised system: the Flemish experience. *Promot Educ,* 2(2-3):91-97.

Ministerie van de Vlaamse Gemeenschap (1997). *Vlaamse regionale indicatoren [Flemish regional indicators].* Brussels, Ministerie van de Vlaamse Gemeenschap, Administratie Planning en Statistiek [Ministry of the Flemish Community, Administration for Planning and Statistics].

Nutbeam D, Wise M (1996). Planning for health for all: international experience in setting health goals and targets. *Health Promotion International,* 11:219-227.

Rada J, Ratima M, Howden-Chapman P (1999). Evidence-based purchasing of health promotion: methodology for reviewing evidence. *Health Promotion International,* 14:177-187.

Rychetnik L et al. (2004). A glossary for evidence based public health. *J Epidemiol Community Health,* 58(7):538-545.

Scheerder G, Van den Broucke S (2001) *A computer application to monitor local health promotion interventions.* Annual Meeting of the European Public Health Association, December 2001. Brussels.

Van Casteren V, Leurquin P (1992). Eurosentinel - Development of an international sentinel network of general practioners. *Meth Inform Med,* 31:147-52.

Van den Broucke S, Denekens J (1999). De Vlaamse gezondheidsdoelstellingen: een richtsnoer voor preventie [The Flemish health targets: guidelines for prevention]. *Tijdschrift voor Geneeskunde,* 55(17):1195-1206.

Van den Broucke S, Stevens V (2001). Beleid en organisatie van de gezondheidspromotie in Vlaanderen [Policy and organization of health promotion in Flanders]. In: Stevens V, Van den Broucke S eds. *Gezondheidspromotie: Tien Jaar Gezondheidspromotie in Vlaanderen [Health Promotion: Ten Years of Health Promotion in Flanders].* Leuven/Apeldoorn, Garant: 31-46.

van Herten LM, Gunning-Schepers LJ (2000). Targets as a tool in health policy. Part I: lessons learned. *Health Policy,* 53(1):1-11.

van Herten LM, Gunning-Schepers LJ (2000). Targets as a tool in health policy. Part II: guidelines for application. *Health Policy,* 53(1):13-23.

Vanweddingen M (2004). *VRIND 2003. Vlaamse regionale indicatoren [Flemish regional indicators, 2003].* Brussels, Ministerie van de Vlaamse Gemeenschap, Administratie Planning en Statistiek [Ministry of the Flemish Community, Administration for Planning and Statistics].

Vereecken C, Maes L, Van De Mieroop E (1998). Jongeren en gezondheidsgedrag in Vlaanderen [Youth and health behaviour in Flanders]. In: Aelvoet W, Capet F, Vanoverloop J, eds. *Gezondheidsindicatoren 1996 [Health Indicators 1996].* Brussels, Ministerie van de Vlaamse Gemeenschap [Ministry of the Flemish Community, Administration for Planning and Statistics]: 78-87.

Vlaams Minister van Welzijn and Volksgezondheid en Gezin (2004). *Beleidsnota Welzijn, Volksgezondheid en Gezin 2004-2009 [Policy document on wellness, public health and family 2004-2005].* Brussels, Vlaams Minister van Welzijn, Volksgezondheid en Gezin [Flemish Minister of Wellbeing, Health and Family].

Vlaams Parlement (2005). *Handelingen. Commissievergadering Welzijn, Volksgezondheid en Gezin [Flemish Parliament, Minutes of the Commission on Wellness, Public Health and Family],* Sitting of 15 March 2005, Brussels, Flemish Parliament.

WHO Regional Office for Europe (1985). *Targets for Health for All. Targets in support of the European regional strategy for health for all.* Copenhagen, WHO Regional Office for Europe.

WHO Regional Office for Europe (1999). *Health21: the Health for All policy framework for the WHO European Region.* Copenhagen, WHO Regional Office for Europe.

Chapter 8

France: Targeting Investment in Health

Valérie Paris, Dominique Polton[8]

Historical background

Health targets have a rather recent history in the formulation of policies in France, with one possible exception. The Planning, Programming and Budgeting System (PPBS) of the 1970s could be seen as the first step in defining and implementing health targets. In particular, the perinatal health plan launched in the early 1970s is considered exemplary and often cited as an example of a very successful planning process. This had a quantitative target – to decrease the perinatal mortality rate from 24 to 18 per 1000. Another objective was to diminish the frequency of children born with disabilities. Operational programmes were defined: vaccination against rubella; strengthening of perinatal monitoring; improving conditions for delivery; enhancing neonatal resuscitation; better staff training. The perinatal death rate decreased dramatically in the 1970s but it is not clear to what extent this was attributable to the plan. However, this remained an isolated example and health targets basically disappeared from the policy process for the next 20 years.

In fact, the French health system has features that are not the most amenable to management by objectives. Modelled on the Bismarckian type (although in some ways a hybrid) it has a strong tradition of state intervention, unlike the self-governing social insurance system in Germany. As in most Bismarckian systems, curative care is emphasized over prevention and public health issues do not generally have a high priority. The activity of the health-care system is

[8] The authors wish to thank Alain Fontaine, from the General Health Directorate, Ministry of Health, for all the information provided. Authors are responsible for all opinions and any possible mistakes.

viewed as the consequence of individual supply and demand. The high value given to freedom of choice and individual responsiveness, and the freedom granted to physicians in independent practice, conflicts with both a population approach and the idea of organizing the system in order to deliver targeted achievements.

Another feature common to other social insurance systems – difficulty in controlling expenditure – regularly puts the issues of cost control and sickness-fund deficits very high on the political agenda, at the expense of other public policy objectives. We will see below that one of the reasons for the rather slow implementation of the Public Health Law enacted in July 2004 is the greater priority given to health insurance reform.

Despite these issues health targets have gained growing legitimacy in France over the last ten years, in common with growing public health concerns.[9]

The first comprehensive set of health targets was proposed by the High Committee on Public Health (Haut Comité de la Santé Publique, HCSP) created in 1991. Health in France was its first report, issued in 1994[10] and publicized widely. This showed that France had very good results in terms of life expectancy after 65 (partly attributable to the effectiveness of curative care) but premature mortality was higher than in most European countries. Building on this observation, the High Committee recommended the adoption of specific objectives to address a set of health problems. It proposed quantitative targets for 14 health problems considered as priorities (road injuries, cancers, cardiovascular diseases, mental health, disabilities, etc.) as well as health determinants (excessive drinking, tobacco use, deprivation and social exclusion, access to health care). Each target was formulated in terms of outcomes to be achieved by 2000 and proposed indicators to monitor progress. For the implementation process, the High Committee emphasized the mobilization of actors, fostering of public debate and the decentralization of implementation to the regional level as key elements of success.

Although highly publicized, the recommendations of the High Committee did not translate into national policy. Pilot initiatives were used to experiment with strategic planning of health interventions and were formalized by the 1996 law reforming the health-care system.[11] Health conferences were created

---

[9] Driven partly by the AIDS epidemic and the infected blood scandal in the 1990s. Nevertheless, this impetus oriented the development of public health towards health surveillance and security. Several independent agencies have achieved much in these areas since the beginning of the 1990s.

[10] A first report was delivered to the Minister of Health in December 1992.

at national and regional levels. The regional conference was a setting in which stakeholders debated local health problems and offered a way to reach consensus on regional priorities which can then be translated into operational regional health programmes (programmes régionaux de santé, PRS) that foster partnerships between all actors involved.

In addition, the 1998 social exclusion act emphasized specific programmes focused on access to health care and health prevention among deprived populations (programmes régionaux d'accès à la prévention et aux soins, PRAPS). By January 2004, 106 regional health programmes (including those focused on deprived populations) had been launched, concerning about 20 health issues (i.e. 3-4 in each region).

All this represented an innovative and, in many respects, experimental process in the French context. The general approach was bottom-up, based on partnership and mobilization of diverse actors, breaking with traditional sectoral public provision (hospitals, physicians in private practice, etc.) and relying on regulatory instruments. The staff of regional administrations received specific training on the methodology and practice of strategic planning. The role of regional health conferences as instruments of democratic debate on the regional scene, their structure and the role that users should play in the process have been the subject of numerous debates.

Evaluations conducted after five to ten years at national and regional level have shown mixed results. The actual implementation of the PRS has often been disappointing, identifying weaknesses such as imprecise targets, lack of project-management capacity and an absence of evaluation. Enthusiasm seems to have declined at the end of the 1990s. Evaluation of the PRAPS programmes showed the same shortcomings but also identified some positive aspects such as implementing some innovative responses to the needs of deprived populations. Both the PRS and the PRAPS have contributed to:

• promoting and disseminating new practices; decompartmentalizing institutions in a field where numerous actors tend to intervene in an uncoordinated manner;
• transforming the vision of public intervention and the roles of the various actors involved;
• developing a common culture of public health.

---

[11] The rhetoric developed by the High Committee on Public Health and the subsequent pilot experiments to test regional conference and strategic planning in some regions were strongly influenced by a few very active representatives of the public health community within the Ministry of Health.

These may be the main results of this first generation of public health programmes, rather more than their actual impact on the health problems concerned.

Meanwhile, there have been increasing calls for a more strongly affirmed public health policy at the national level. This has been especially true since 1996 when parliament assumed responsibility for defining the expenditure ceiling for the sickness fund for the following year. The lack of debate on health targets compared badly with the interest in financial targets, appearing more and more as an imbalance in the democratic process.

From this perspective, the government that came to power in 2002 launched an ambitious project to design and implement a public health plan. It initiated a new process to formulate and implement health targets, which is analysed in the following section. The Cancer Plan, clearly the most structured and comprehensive approach to implement health targets, is examined in the third section.

The Public Health Policy Act (PHPA) of 9 August 2004: from conception to implementation

Content of the PHPA

The PHPA adopted on 9 August 2004 affirms the state's role and responsibility in public health policy. It defines the scope, process of elaboration and instruments of implementation of this policy at the national and regional level. Parliament is given responsibility for voting every five years on the public health policy objectives proposed by the government. The PHPA states that regional public health plans must be consistent with these national objectives and created a new regional institution to implement them. It also addresses research and training in public health, with the creation of a new school of public health. Finally, it states that the implementation of the law will be monitored on a yearly basis and evaluated after five years.

Apart from these institutional changes, the PHPA enacts regulations on health determinants such as nutrition, alcohol, tobacco use (e.g. banning food and drink dispensers in high schools; introducing rules on food advertising , etc.) and the environment (water, lead, etc.). As a consequence of the heatwave of

---

[12] Apart from all these measures pertaining to public health policy, the PHPA contains provisions for creating professional associations for some health professions and defining their competencies. It also transposes the provisions of the European Directives on clinical trials into French law.

August 2003, the PHPA makes some provisions to enhance alert and response systems during health emergencies.[12]

Finally, an appendix to the law sets 100 national public health objectives to be achieved within 5 years[13] and announces 5 strategic national plans for 2004-2008: on cancer; to reduce the health impact of violence (road injuries being the President's main priority); on health and environment; to improve the quality of life of persons with chronic diseases; and for rare diseases.

The definition of targets: mobilizing expertise

The method selected to define health targets relied formally on several types of contribution. Regional health authorities (DRASS) organized consultations between October and November 2002, with the following goals:

- To identify the main health issues for each region and to review the results of regional health policies from previous years;
- To report viewpoints of the main health actors on the distribution of competencies between national and regional authorities in public health policy;
- To report on their views on appropriate ways to prioritize health targets.

The French Public Health Association (Société Française de Santé Publique, SFSP) was in charge of synthesizing the 26 regional contributions. These were presented in its report of 13 February 2003 (Oberlé et al. 2003).

At the national level, the National Technical Group for the Definition of Public Health Objectives (Groupe Technique National de Définition des Objectifs de Santé, GTNDO) was created in November 2002. Its mission was to propose a set of objectives defined as "quantifiable and realistic" targets. The group comprised representatives of 20 institutions (health insurance funds, departments of the Ministry of Health, health agencies, INSERM, statistical offices and centres) and about 60 experts, mainly epidemiologists, public health physicians and clinicians. Medical experts were assigned responsibility to report on possible strategies to tackle the main problems for their own specialty (related to determinants of health or to diseases) and to assess the effectiveness of these strategies. At this stage, there were no representatives from patients' associations or professional organizations. They were consulted later in the process.

---

[13] The Public Health Plan and all documents related to debates in parliament are available on the assembly's web site: Public Health Policy Act of August 9, 2004 (legislative dossier): www.assemblee-nat.fr/12/dossiers/sante_publique.asp (the table containing the 100 objectives is in the PDF file).

A subgroup of the GTNDO was charged with proposing a method to define the final set of objectives, i.e. prioritize within a larger set of objectives. This group was managed by the Ministry's Department of Public Health and was composed of qualified experts with backgrounds in public health, health economics or management. The group was posed the following questions. What criteria should be used to define public health objectives? Should we choose objectives that maximize health gain? Reduce the costs of illnesses? Maximize population satisfaction? Address health inequalities? Should we adopt a rights-based or an evidence-based approach? Should we focus on diseases with high and increasing prevalence?

This group met regularly between October 2002 and January 2003. During the process, the National Institute for Prevention and Health Education (Institut National de Prévention et d'Education pour la Santé, INPES) produced a document compiling 415 propositions of actions explicitly or implicitly formulated in experts' reports and giving any available evidence about their effectiveness. The High Committee on Public Health was asked to synthesize its previous reports on health status and to validate objectives proposed by the GTNDO. The Department of Public Health of the Ministry of Health was involved deeply throughout the process.

The GTNDO submitted its report on 10 March 2003 (Direction Générale de la Santé & INSERM 2003). This supplied an inventory of available scientific evidence relating to 70 health problems, their determinants and the public health strategies for responding to them. These health problems were identified from two sources: (1) health issues outlined by the High Committee on Public Health were systematically taken into account; (2) health issues that WHO reported to be responsible for more than 0.2% of the burden of disease in its European Region. Health problems for which effective strategies exist were added to the list. Thus, the main criterion was the burden of disease.

This report also presented quantified objectives, defined as: "objectives which could be reached in absence of constraints in available resources". These were established according to two principles.

- Where France ranked poorly among European countries in 2000, the objective was to reach the European average in 2005.
- Where France ranked high, the objective was to maintain this level through 2008 in spite of demographic evolution.

The more ambitious objective was selected when no comparative data were available.

The report was posted on the Ministry's web site for public consultation. Hundreds of responses were recorded, mainly comments and suggestions from medical experts outside the GTNDO or from medical societies. Some of these were taken into account in the final version of the report. The Minister of Health and the Government finalized a list of 100 objectives to be proposed in the appendix to the PHPA.

The objectives received little debate in parliament – due to their large number and the previous efforts to reach consensus. A few questioned the likelihood of achieving the large number of objectives and the absence of prioritization. There were a few comments about the realism of some isolated indicators (for instance 'reduce by 30% pollution exposure'). Finally, some deputies questioned the status of the appendix in that (unlike the PHPA itself) this text had no normative value. Citizens were not able to challenge regulatory measures that conflicted with the objectives. The government dismissed this objection since it was clear that this appendix only aimed to present a strategic direction for the next five years.

Formulation of health targets in the PHPA

The 100 objectives (or targets) appended to the PHPA are of different types (Table 8-1).

Concrete measures to achieve these targets do not feature in the PHPA (with some exceptions), since the essential aim is to establish the basis for future elaboration of public health policies. Strategic plans and other programmes are planned (or already in force) to implement these targets (see Cancer Plan).

Table 8-1 *Types of targets in the PHPA*

Targets expressed in terms of reduction of mortality or morbidity, for example: reduce by 30% deaths due to chronic hepatitis.
Targets to address the determinants of health – reduce/increase the prevalence of risky/healthy behaviour; reduce pollution (including noise) exposure (at workplace, home or in atmosphere), for example: reduce alcohol consumption per capita by 20%.
Targets to reduce social inequalities in health-care access and health status and to reduce restrictions on activity due to disabilities, for example: increase the life expectancy of disadvantaged people.
Targets for improvement in the health-care process – reduce the prevalence of iatrogenic incidents and antibiotic resistance; improve pain care; increase participation in prevention programmes (e.g. screening); increase compliance with guidelines for certain types of treatment (e.g. diabetes surveillance).
Targets for increased knowledge, better surveillance and the definition of strategies (for instance, a strategy for colorectal cancer screening should be defined within four years).

Policy implementation: the institutional issue

On the whole, the overall efficacy of prevention and health promotion is impaired by the multiplicity of financers, dilution of responsibilities and fragmentation of actors. The historical dual management role of the state and the sickness funds is reflected in a rather complex institutional construction. This reinforces the problem of lack of responsibility and accountability within the French health system. One major goal of the law was thus to clarify the missions of the many institutions responsible for public health (national versus regional level; state versus parastatal, for example: health insurance funds).

First, the PHPA affirms the state's responsibility for defining health targets and implementing public health policies. The state will define national objectives and orientations for public health policies every five years and will account to parliament for the results. At regional level, the state representative (Préfet) is also responsible for the definition of objectives and for the elaboration and implementation of regional public health plans. Parliament is required to vote on health targets every five years in order to guarantee a minimum of consensus and legitimate the actions of the state.

The PHPA created several national institutions with the aim of simplifying and clarifying decision-making. The High Council for Public Health (Haut Conseil de la Santé Publique) was created as a source of expertise to participate in the formulation and definition of health targets and their strategic orientations.[14] In parallel, the interministerial National Committee for Public Health was created to define concrete priorities for prevention and health protection; coordinate the actions of the state and the health insurance funds; and determine evaluation methods.

The PHPA acknowledged the regional level to be the optimal level for the definition and coordination of public health policies. Regional public health plans (plans régional de santé publique, PRSP) must be defined under the authority of the préfet, and a new institution created to ensure coordination between regional stakeholders. The creation of this new regional institution was perhaps the most controversial measure in the PHPA since it was suspected that it would complicate the already fragmented landscape of regional decision-making.

Actually, two institutions were created by the 1996 reform in addition to the Health Ministry's existing regional administrations. Regional hospital agencies (agences régionales. de l'hospitalisation, ARHs) are a joint venture between the

---

[14] Takes over the tasks of the former High Committee on Public Health and several missions of the High Council of Public Hygiene, both now defunct.

state's regional services and those of the health insurance funds, although the state has greater influence. ARHs have responsibility for both planning and financial allocation in the hospital sector. Regional health insurance unions (l'union régionale des caisses d'assurance maladie, URCAMs) are federal structures that combine the three principal schemes (general; agricultural; for the self-employed) within each region. Less operational than the ARHs, they mainly coordinate the risk-management policies of the different sickness funds at the regional level. They have no authority over the regional and local funds. Apart from their involvement in the ARHs, the regional administrations of the Health Ministry have always retained a public health mission.

This complicated institutional landscape has often been criticized as a factor in the compartmentalization of policies, weakness of global regulation and incapacity to tackle health problems in an integrated way. Continuing debate concerns the possibility of merging all institutions into a single regional health agency (agence régionale de santé, ARS) which would have overall responsibility. This was discussed during the preparation of the law but the regional hospitalization agencies argued that they were best equipped to take on responsibilities for public health, and that this would contribute towards the unification of all institutions. This was not the final decision, a new (and additional) institution was created – the Regional Group of Public Health (Groupement regional de santé publique). This is placed squarely under state responsibility as it is a joint venture between the state administration, the ARHs and the URCAMs.

Apart from the growing complexity of the institutional setting, this means that implementation will depend crucially on the ability of these three administrations. Despite rivalries and potential conflicts they must work together and in the same direction. This is a clear weakness that creates a risk of inefficient implementation.

Another important feature is the departure from the previous bottom-up model where regional priorities were defined through regional consultation and debate. The law reintroduces a top-down approach, with national objectives imposed on the regions.

The PHPA maintains two consultative bodies at national and regional levels. The National and Regional Health Conferences comprise representatives of all stakeholders in the health-care system: patients and users; health professionals; local government; health authorities; and humanitarian associations, etc. Regional health conferences are consulted during the development process of regional public health plans and must assess their implementation together with the implementation of the Patients' Rights Act of 2002.

Beyond institutional issues: programmes and budgets

Once health targets and the institutional framework for the implementation of public health policies have been defined, concrete implementation modalities have to be defined further and funds allocated.

As stated in the PHPA, concrete actions are defined in national (such as the Cancer Plan described below) and regional public health plans. Even if national plans set out activities over several years, funding will be determined annually using two instruments. The Social Security Funding Act (SSFA) sets out the income and expenditure of all social security funds (including health insurance) and introduces measures for the organization of health care. The Budget Act defines the state's income and expenditure for all domains of activity (health, education, defence, etc.). Following an important reform in 2001, budget acts now incorporate a performance-based approach. Strategies, objectives and indicators (to measure the achievement of objectives) are defined for each public programme; budgets are allocated by "mission" (combining several programmes) and depend on the results achieved in the previous period.[15] Parliament votes on both the SSFA and the Budget Act, providing the opportunity for a review of the resources allocated to implement health targets.

Assessment of implementation

The PHPA requires its implementation to be assessed annually and the government to report every five years on the impact of its policies on the heath status of the French population. The Parliamentary Office for the Assessment of Health Policy has a mandate to assess the implementation of any health policy and programme at any time. It reported on the implementation of the PHPA in March 2005, six months after its adoption.

The report observed that 68 of the 158 sections of the PHPA were applicable immediately but the remaining sections required new texts (decrees, ministerial orders, administrative circulars). Implementation was especially weak – of the 132 texts that should have been issued, only 7 had been published. The report put forward several explanations for the delay. First, the drafting of these texts assumes consultation and cooperation with numerous actors. Second, the Public Health Department had been heavily engaged in the preparation and implementation of the Health Insurance Act of 13 August

---

[15] This new budgeting process is expected to soften the impact of budget history and ministers' personal negotiating power on budget allocation to ministries. However, it is too early to assess its effectiveness.

2004; clearly a priority of the Minister.[16] The state audit body reports that the drafting of all necessary texts for the implementation of the two Acts represents four years work for the department. Clearly this compromises the achievement of objectives to be met over five years (Cour des Comptes 2004).

In November 2005, the Parliamentary Office for the Assessment of Health Policy published a second report on the implementation of the PHPA. In spite of persisting delays, the report was more optimistic and predicted partial implementation by the end of 2005. In July 2005, a set of indicators to assess the implementation of the 100 health targets of the Public Health Act was developed from collective expertise. This was published in a weighty document (Government of France 2005).

Finally, the production of legislative texts to implement the PHPA was one of the objectives of the Budget Act for 2006.

The Cancer Plan

The Cancer Plan is probably the greatest achievement of the five health plans announced in the PHPA of 2004. In reality, this plan was implemented before the PHPA was adopted by parliament.

In his speech of 14 July 2001, the French President established three high priorities – the fight against cancer; fight against road-traffic injuries; and better integration of people with disabilities within the community. The Cancer Plan was launched in 2003 after a year of preparation.

Preparation

In September 2002, the Health Minister appointed a steering committee on cancer to diagnose the French situation and provide health authorities with recommendations about the best ways to reduce cancer-related mortality in France. The committee comprised 20 members: 7 representatives of 2 departments of the Ministry of Health and 13 doctors and professors of medicine, either practising or involved in research. One of these was the President of the Ligue Nationale Contre le Cancer, the most important private not-for-profit association representing cancer patients, prevention and research. The committee collected many data on cancer incidence, mortality and survival rates and conducted about 80 hearings for physicians and other health professionals, patients' associations and health insurance funds.

---

[16] Although both laws were enacted at the same time, it is also useful to note that the Public Health Law was initiated by the previous Minister of Health.

The report was submitted on 16 January 2003 (Direction Générale de la Santé 2003), with the following conclusions about the French situation. Cancer prevalence has been increasing dramatically in the last 20 years and France has the highest rate of cancer-related mortality in the EU. Primary prevention, early diagnosis and screening are insufficiently developed. In spite of good quality of care that provides a fair survival rate for cancer patients (in comparison with other countries) there are inequalities in accessibility to adequate and high-quality care. Equipment for cancer diagnosis and therapy is still insufficient and access to innovative treatments (drugs and equipment) is inequitable. Access to psychological support and other types of care (such as pain or palliative care) have really improved since previous years but demand is still growing. Current modes of payment for medical services do not support necessary developments in the system. Shortages of health professionals working in oncology are anticipated. Patients with cancer too often experience difficulties at work and in accessing insurance contracts or bank loans; and lack information about their disease and possible treatments.

At the end of this report, the Steering Committee formulated "10+1" recommendations for action to fight cancer (Table 8-2).

The eleventh recommendation called for the creation of a National Institute of Cancer (INCa) to stimulate and coordinate research activities; provide high-level expertise to professionals and to health authorities; monitor and evaluate the performance of cancer treatments and implement new technologies; provide public information about clinical trials, available

Table 8-2 *Recommendations for action to fight cancer*

Improve the epidemiological information system.
Reinforce prevention policies, especially at the local level with an emphasis on the reduction of tobacco and alcohol consumption and on the promotion of appropriate diets.
Stimulate the development of screening.
Improve the quality of care through structural changes likely to produce better coordination of care.
Reform the payment of cancer treatments to public and private hospitals and to ambulatory providers.
Increase the amount of medical equipment and funding for new drugs.
Develop support and information for patients.
Promote social inclusion of cancer patients.
Create conditions for a dramatic development of research on cancer.
Increase the number of specialized professionals in oncology.

treatments, social benefits and patients' rights; and promote the dissemination of French research throughout Europe.

Content

The Cancer Plan was launched 24 March 2003, i.e. only three months after being recommended. Its main objective was to reduce cancer-related mortality by 20% within five years. A large set of operational goals (70) to achieve this ultimate objective were defined and presented in six priority chapters.

The initial plan announced a total funding of €640 million to 2007. This was allocated to prevention and screening (13%); care coordination and patient support (21%); facilities and care upgrades (16%); access to innovative treatments (32%); and research and training (18%). It also announced the creation of 1700 nursing and technical staff, 500 physicians, 400 patient-support staff and 660 posts in other categories.

Implementation and monitoring

The Prime Minister appointed a national project task force to work under the authority of the Minister of Health in order to implement and monitor the

Table 8-3 *Priorities in the French Cancer Plan*

Increase primary prevention through a better knowledge on cancer causes; the fight against smoking, against work- and environment-related cancer; and the promotion of pro-health attitudes.

Improve screening, especially for breast, colorectal and cervical cancer; improve early detection of melanoma; and provide better access to testing for inherited forms of cancer.

Improve quality of care and focus care on patients, i.e. ensure more equity in access to the best treatments; strengthen coordination between professionals and between home and hospital care; improve access to information for patients and more attention to patients' expectations; guarantee access to diagnostic and therapeutic innovation by expanding the number of diagnostic and therapeutic facilities and increasing the funds dedicated to expensive new drugs.

Provide more humane and more comprehensive social-support structures by creating mechanisms to help cancer patients to remain at work; increase patients' access to loans and insurance; encourage home health care and possibilities for parents to stay close to hospitalized children; provide patients with psychological support.

Enhance training of professionals by including oncology education in the first stages of nursing and medical curricula.

Develop research by creating regional cancer foci and a National Cancer Institute.

plan. The Mission Interministérielle pour la Lutte contre le Cancer (MILC) was created by a decree of 7 May 2003. Until the creation of the National Institute of Cancer in 2006, the MILC produced annual reports on the implementation of the Plan, publicly available on its web site (http://www.plancancer.fr). A set of key indicators was used to plan regional and national monitoring mechanisms. A first set of indicators defined in 2003 was refined and included in the set of 100 objectives and related indicators adopted in the PHPA passed on the 9 August 2004. It is worth noting that communication about the Cancer Plan, its implementation and its annual assessments is considered outstanding in the French context.

Space does not permit a detailed description of all aspects of the Cancer Plan. Therefore, the focus is on some examples of policy instruments used to implement targets within it. Six broad strategies were identified.

1. Strengthen the state's engagement through earmarked funding, performance-based budgeting and involvement of several ministries.
2. Use regulatory instruments such as legislation and economic incentives.
3. Mobilize expertise at different stages of the process.
4. Educate the public.
5. Create incentives to ensure professional involvement.
6. Develop a hierarchy of care and pooling of resources at the regional level.

Strengthening the state's engagement

As explained above, some of the Cancer Plan's objectives are included in the 100 objectives defined in the PHPA and/or in objectives set in other national plans implemented later. For instance, the Cancer Plan includes a target to improve the diet of the population, essentially through educational campaigns and enhanced consumer information. In reality, this goal is the main target of the existing National Nutrition and Health Programme (defined for 2001-2005 then renewed for the following five years). Moreover, the Cancer Plan's general target builds on specific targets defined in the PHPA (reduce obesity prevalence by 20%, the number of people eating too few fruits and vegetables from 60% to 45%, and salt consumption to 8 mg/day per capita; stop the increase of obesity prevalence in children).

Similarly, the intention to act on occupational risks is addressed further by the National Health at the Workplace Plan (2005–2009), presented 17 February 2005. This contains eight strategic objectives, one of which is to reduce exposure thresholds to carcinogenic agents. Measures to act on environmental-related risk factors are also part of the National Health and Environment Plan (2004–2008) (Ministère de la santé et de la solidarité 2004) – reduce exposures at the workplace; reinforce French capacity to assess risks linked to the use of chemical substances; develop new methods to assess environmental and societal determinants of health; reduce emissions of toxic industrial substances; and enhance knowledge on the quality of indoor air.

In addition to these three public health plans, throughout its 70 propositions the Cancer Plan refers to measures which have been (or will be adopted) in other pieces of legislation, such as annual social security funding acts or specific administrative documents (circulaires). Although confusing at first sight, since identical objectives are attributed to several national health programmes, this overlap provides specific benefits. It formally acknowledges the link between cancer (health) and environmental factors. Also, it supports cooperation among all stakeholders in order to define operational goals. More specifically, it ensures coordination between government services.

The state's engagement in the fight against cancer is confirmed by the budgets allocated to the Cancer Plan. As stated in the Budget Act for 2006, the funding for cancer increased from €5 million in 2002 to €96.5 million in 2006. It now accounts for one quarter of all expenditure that the state allocates to public health.[17] According to the new framework of the Budget Act, objectives and indicators are defined to measure the efficiency of public expenditures in the cancer domain (Table 8-4).

As proposed in the Hospital 2007 plan, new equipment for cancer treatment and diagnosis will be purchased, existing equipment will be modernized and access to new technology will be made more equitable. Specific targets were set for 2007: the installation of 112 new linear accelerators, 69 computerized tomography (CT) scanners and 68 magnetic resonance imaging (MRI) machines; and to have one positron emission tomography (PET) scanner in each region.

Mobilizing expertise to increase knowledge

Medical expertise is not only deeply embedded in the preparation of the Cancer Plan but also features throughout its implementation. For instance, the first target is to achieve better knowledge of the causes of cancer. The Institute for Public Health Surveillance (InVS) is responsible for epidemiological surveillance of cancer; i.e. to develop cancer registries linked to mortality data and data from other sources (hospitals, health insurance funds, etc.) to provide data on incidence, survival and the process of care.

---

[17] These expenditures do not include health-insurance fund spending on prevention, screening and care.

Another objective is a better knowledge of risk factors, especially those associated with the environment or occupations. To achieve this target, the PHPA appointed the InVS to assemble data on work injuries, occupational diseases and other information related to work and health. Other measures figure in the National Health and Environment Plan or in the framework agreement signed between health and labour ministries in February 2004. The latter strengthens surveillance to develop a better knowledge of carcinogenic substances and enhance occupational protection. This mission is also assigned to InVS but the Health at the Workplace Plan also establishes an independent public agency charged with providing independent expertise on risk assessment in the workplace.

Scientific expertise is also deeply involved in the strategies related to the target of the second priority chapter – to improve screening for several types of cancer. For instance, further evaluation to establish strategies for screening for colorectal and cervical cancers. The programme for colorectal cancer

Table 8-4 *Objectives and indicators for the Public Health and Prevention Programme in the performance-based Budget Act for 2006*

Objectives	Related indicators
1. Write and publish with the least delays legislative texts necessary for the implementation of health laws and transposition of EU Directives	Number and percentage of texts published/number of texts to be published
2. Improve citizens' participation in the definition, implementation and monitoring of public health policy	Citizen associations' participation rate in bodies in which they are expected to participate Percentage of subsidized associations whose activities have been assessed
3. Enhance knowledge about health status of the population by reducing delays in processing death certificates by the National Institute for Health and Medical Research (INSERM)	Average delay in processing death certificates
4. Reduce the prevalence of addictive behaviours	Annual per capita alcohol consumption above 15 years Prevalence of daily tobacco consumption in general population, for men, women and young people Prevalence of cannabis consumption at various ages

Continued

Objectives	Related indicators
5. Reduce exposure to some environmental risks	Output of lead-poisoning screening (number of intoxicated children/number of screened children, as an indicator of good targeting of screening)
	Number of cases of carbon monoxide exposure
6. Encourage behaviours likely to prevent HIV/AIDS transmission	Percentage of young people 15-26 that used a condom in their last sexual contact
	Percentage of young people 18-24 that used a condom in their last sexual contact, by gender
	Rate of recognition of HIV-prevention campaigns in general population and in targeted groups (migrants, homosexuals)
7. Improve breast cancer screening	Participation rate in targeted population screening (objective is 80%, with earlier screening in cancer history).
	Unit costs of breast cancer screening
	Ratio of mammographies undertaken in established screening programme in all mammographies (incl. individual screenings) in women 50-74
	Actual breakdown of funds allocated to the Cancer Plan compared to initial planned breakdown
	Indicator to be built to assess the coordination function of the National Cancer Institute

screening, evaluated in 22 départements, was assessed in order to define a national strategy for 2007. The evaluation involved a comparative assessment of two tests (Hemoccult II and Magstream). For cervical cancer, the French National Agency for Accreditation and Evaluation in Healthcare (ANAES) assessed the benefits of the human papillomavirus test but did not recommend its systematic use in association with the Pap test.

The main targets for improvement in cancer care were quality enhancement and easier and more equitable access to treatments. Scientific expertise is deeply involved through the production of guidelines and recommendations by medical societies, ANAES (replaced in 2004 by the High Authority for Health) or by the National Federation of French Cancer Centres (replaced by the National Cancer Institute).

Finally, an important feature of the Cancer Plan is to strengthen research and restore France's high position in international and European cancer-research networks. To achieve this goal the PHPA called for the creation of a national cancer institute. INCa was finally established in May 2005 with the mission to stimulate research by establishing research programmes, allocating grants and encouraging synergies between research and care.

To conclude, the mobilization of expertise addresses three broad objectives – to increase knowledge; promote high-quality and/or cost-effective practices; and stimulate medical research.

Use of regulatory instruments: legislation and economic incentives

Legislative and economic instruments are used mainly in the field of primary prevention. Almost all of those in existence were introduced by the PHPA of 2004.

A financial incentive was the first measure used to achieve the fourth target of the Cancer Plan (reduction of tobacco consumption): cigarette prices increased by 42% between January 2003 and January 2004. This was accompanied by a set of legal constraints – sales to young people under 16 are now forbidden and warning labels on cigarette packages have been strengthened. The PHPA enhanced the means available to enforce the provisions of the Evin law that ban smoking in public areas, allowing more professionals to enforce them and increasing fines for contravention. The PHPA also ratified the WHO Framework Convention on Tobacco Control, which contains provisions relating to tobacco prices, taxes, promotion, labelling and packaging, among others.

The Cancer Plan also increased controls in order to reinforce the ban on alcohol promotion. However, in this case, the industry's active lobbying resulted in the adoption of an amendment to the Evin law. The text that liberalized the promotion of wine was adopted on 13 October 2004 (102/114 votes in favour), only two months after the same assembly had adopted the PHPA.

The PHPA also introduced new legal constraints to promote healthy nutrition. Manufacturers of drinks or food containing added sugar, salt or sugar substitutes must insert warnings about health risks in their promotional messages unless they pay a tax (1.5% of expenditure on promotion). This revenue is allocated to INPES to promote healthy nutrition habits. As from 1 September 2005, it also banned drinks and food vending machines in schools.

Regulatory instruments are used less often for purposes other than prevention. One exception is the Plan's call for further extensions of the Belorgey convention which facilitates bank loans to cancer patients.

Education of the public

The Cancer Plan's second set of targets aims to promote healthy attitudes by reducing tobacco and alcohol consumption and promoting healthy nutrition and physical activities. The dissemination of educational messages is the key instrument to achieve these goals, in certain cases linked to financial incentives and the enforcement of legal constraints.

The Health and Education Ministries collaborated to implement public health programmes in schools, raising consciousness among young people about risks linked to tobacco and cannabis consumption. The INPES launched several campaigns, such as the Smoke-free Hospitals and Smoke-free Schools programmes. Media campaigns were designed to challenge the positive image of tobacco and raise awareness of its risks. There is a clear willingness to change the social norms on tobacco consumption.

Efforts to reduce alcohol consumption essentially focus on information campaigns launched by INPES. These aim to inform the public about risks related to immoderate consumption of alcohol; modifying masculine representations of alcohol; promoting total abstinence during pregnancy; and enhancing the dialogue between patients and professionals. In 2003, several television campaigns called attention to the health risks related to harmful alcohol consumption. Advertisements in the press associated masculine values with moderate alcohol consumption – Bois moins si tu es un homme.

The Cancer Plan reinforced the existing National Nutrition and Health Programme (defined for 2001-2005) (Ministère de la santé et de la solidarité 2001). In 2003, INPES disseminated nutrition guides for patients and professionals and launched a national campaign promoting the consumption of at least five portions of fruit and vegetables per day and greater physical activity. Similarly, the prevention of skin cancer relies essentially on educational campaigns informing people about health risks related to sun or artificial ultraviolet exposure.

Information campaigns were launched to encourage participation in screening programmes. For instance, an ambitious 80% target was set for participation in breast cancer screening (estimated at 30% in 2003 with huge variations from 11% to 70% between départements). Several campaigns have been launched at national and local level, including television spots. The PHPA called for specific programmes to focus on women reluctant to participate (isolated, disabled, deprived). This has been partly achieved by the production of films or tapes for people with visual or hearing impairments and the translation of brochures for immigrants. Patients' and women's associations are involved actively in this information campaign.

Apart from general information, the Plan also placed emphasis on the information given to cancer patients, from informing them of the cancer diagnosis to explaining treatment options. A hotline Cancer Info Service was created to provide more information and support, and information kiosks are being placed in public areas (shopping centres, etc.). Involvement between hospitals and patient associations are promoted through formal agreements. Finally, the Cancer Plan web site was created in February 2004.

Incentives to obtain professional involvement

Cancer screening in France essentially relies on independent practitioners. The challenge is to find incentives to encourage them to participate in formal screening programmes. Patients have no real financial incentive to participate in formal programmes since individual screening is possible at any time (with the agreement of a physician) and is generally free.[18]

If the main objective of the breast cancer screening programme is to improve the effectiveness of prevention activities, clearly it must limit anarchic practices by avoiding useless or redundant examinations, concentrating on effective prevention and increasing the quality of screening. Since January 2004, screening programmes have been extended to all départements: every woman between 50 and 74 is now invited to benefit from free screening every two years. Breast cancer screening programmes are implemented by management structures in each département which send invitations to targeted women. Examinations are performed by independent professionals (90% of screenings) and financed jointly by general councils and health insurance funds. Radiologists are involved in the programmes according to formal agreements based on quality standards. In addition, the radiologists' trade union has cooperated in the creation of an observatory to gather and analyse data on screening as a means of quality assurance.

In other cases, the professional fee schedule had to be amended to include new procedures. For instance, the evaluation of colorectal cancer screening required the resolution of problems with the payment of physicians and the posting of Hemoccult tests. Similarly, the development of cervical cancer screening was encouraged by including the HPV test in the professionals' fee schedule since December 2003 and reimbursing when there are suspicious results from the Pap test since January 2004.

For cancer care, budgets for very expensive treatments will be isolated in the

---

[18] Until now, copayments were always reimbursed by complementary insurances for those covered (92% of population).

DRG-linked hospital payment system in order to improve access to innovative medicines in hospitals.

Coordination of care

The organization of cancer care has always been a priority in the regional five-year plans for the provision of care (schémas régionaux d'organization sanitaires, SROS). The Cancer Plan acknowledges the benefit of the regional tier in the organization of high-quality care so cancer will remain a priority of the SROS. In addition, cancer-related activities will be more explicitly regulated by regional authorities[19] and submitted to the Regional Hospital Agency for authorization. Hospitals will be linked in a hierarchical structure and designated as reference, specialized or participating centres, according to the treatments available.

Cancer networks will be created at the regional level to coordinate regional structures; share information on outcomes; and pool resources and competencies. The constitution of regional foci aims to ensure equal access to innovation and highly specialized equipment at this level.

Inside hospitals, cooperation between professionals and communication with patients will be formalized in several ways. Coordination centres (Centres de Coordination en Cancérologie or 3Cs) will be created in each hospital to harmonize the activities of all professionals and develop customized care pathways for each patient (programme personnalisé de soins or PPS).

Conclusion

French public health policy has been extensively remodelled in recent years. It is probably too early to make a complete assessment of the impact of the reforms, but it is possible to draw some conclusions from recent experiences.

First, the new public health policy is characterized by health targets formulated by consensus; widespread mobilization of medical expertise; greater legitimacy gained by parliamentary approval of strategies and budgets; and the consultation of citizens' representatives during the elaboration of public health plans.

Second, the implementation of health targets rests upon strategies that involve stakeholders at different levels. Cooperation between state institutions is

---

[19] ARHs already regulated activities on a case-per-case basis through individual agreements with hospitals, but without much accountability to regional stakeholders and other hospitals.

formalized by the creation of the interministerial committee and the elaboration of strategic plans involving several ministries.

Third, the explicit and public mobilization of expertise is a core element of the new public health policies. Beyond the definition of targets, experts are involved in the definition of public health strategies in order to promote cost-effective, high-quality practices. This movement is not just observable in public health; it represents a general trend in the health-care sector.

Other, less new, instruments are used for the implementation of targets but the emphasis on public education is noteworthy.

Finally, monitoring of the implementation of public health strategies is increasingly influenced by the new principles of accountability observed in other public domains. However, it remains to be assessed to what extent so many targets can be taken into account in actual policy formulation.

REFERENCES

Cour des Comptes (2004). *Rapport public annuel 2004*. Paris, Cour des Comptes.

Direction Générale de la Santé (2003). *Rapport de la Commission d'Orientation sur le Cancer*. Paris, Ministre de la Santé, de la Jeunesse et des Sports.

Direction Générale de la Santé & INSERM (2003). *Rapport du GTNDO. Analyse des connaissances disponibles sur des problèmes de santé sélectionnés, leurs déterminants et les stratégies de santé publique – Définition d'objectifs*. Paris, Direction Générale de la Santé & INSERM.

Government of France (2005). *Indicateurs de suivi de l'atteinte des 100 objectifs du rapport annexé à la Loi du 9 août 2004 relative à la politique de santé publique*. Paris, Ministère de l'Emploi, de la Cohésion Sociale et du Logement, Ministère de la Santé et de la Solidarité.

Ministère de la Santé et de la Solidarité (2001). *Program National Nutrition Santé 2001-2005*. Paris, Ministère de la Santé et de la Solidarité.

Ministère de la Santé et de la Solidarité (2004). *Program National Santé Environnement 2004-2008*. Paris, Ministère de la Santé et de la Solidarité.

Oberlé D, Chambaud L, Brodin M (2003). *Synthèse des 26 consultations régionales dans le cadre de la préparation de la Loi d'orientation en santé publique, Rapport élaboré par la société française de santé publique à la demande du Directeur Général de la Santé*. Paris, Société Française de Santé Publique.

Chapter 9

Germany: Targets in a Federal System

Matthias Wismar, Barbara Philippi, Hildegard Klus

Introduction

Today, health targets play an established role in German health policy. Federal health targets were established in 2003 and most of the Länder have either adopted health targets or been influenced by the process (GVG 2007). Health targets also play a role in some health programmes. The disease management programmes (DMPs) launched in 2003 implicitly set targets for patients, providers, sickness funds and at the level of the entire programme (Joos et al. 2005). In addition, health targets are included in the pending prevention act, backed by a budgetary allocation of € 250 million. This was first tabled in 2005 but only reintroduced to Parliament in 2007 (Bundesministerium für Gesundheit 2007).

Health targets have had a fluid history as the focus has moved constantly between the federal and regional levels. Hopes that both would work jointly to develop complementary targets were frustrated. The federal government, while supporting the formulation of national health targets, has given only ambiguous support for implementation, but the process has moved forward under the momentum of regional efforts where the process has been much less politicized.

The future of health targets at the federal level remains unclear. Although the federal government has withdrawn financing, the programme infrastructure is being supported by stakeholders that have been working together for several years (Klus et al. 2007). There are also questions about the future of the DMPs, caught up in the debate about health-care reform. The proposed prevention act has been subject to fierce political and general controversy.

This chapter starts with a review of the emergence of health targets in Germany and an overview of their implementation. Subsequently, there is an examination of the efforts of the federal and regional governments (and other players) to use health targets to exert influence and provide adequate health intelligence to support them. Finally, there is a summary of the lessons learned.

The emergence of health targets in Germany

Health targets have emerged gradually in Germany since the early 1980s, permeating all levels of government and some sickness funds. At the federal level, a report commissioned by the Ministry of Health to identify health priorities was published in 1987 (Weber et al. 1987) and updated after unification in 1990 (Weber et al. 1990). The report was meant to lay the basis for German health targets. However, a combination of political resistance and the challenges posed by German unification led to the failure of the initiative (Wismar and Busse 2000). A second process of target definition, again commissioned by the Federal Ministry of Health, eventually gave rise to national health targets in 2003 (Gesellschaft für Versicherungswissenschaft und -gestaltung (GVG) e.V 2003).

Between the failure of the first federal initiative and the success of the second, the Länder started to define health targets. Today 10 out of 16 Länder have experience with health targets.

Hamburg: first tentative attempts to introduce health targets in 1992 (Behörde für Arbeit Gesundheit und Soziales Freie und Hansestadt Hamburg [Hamburg Authority for Work Health and Social Affairs] 1992), developed further in 1995 (Behörde für Arbeit Gesundheit und Soziales Freie und Hansestadt Hamburg [Hamburg Authority for Work Health and Social Affairs] 1995).

North Rhine-Westphalia: adopted 10 health targets in 1995 (Ministerium für Arbeit Soziales und Gesundheit des Landes Nordrhein-Westfalen [Ministry for Work Social Affairs and Health of North Rhine-Westphalia] 1995), updated in 2005 (Ministerium für Gesundheit Soziales Frauen und Familie des Landes NRW [Ministry for Work Social Affairs and Health of North Rhine-Westphalia] 2005).

Berlin: health targets developed in 1996 (Bergmann et al. 1996), never achieved political endorsement due to changes in the composition of the Senate.

Schleswig-Holstein: health targets defined in 1997 (Ministerium für Arbeit Gesundheit und Soziales des Landes Schleswig-Holstein [Ministry for Work Health and Social Affairs of Schleswig-Holstein] 1997), updated in 2001 and 2003 (Landesregierung Schleswig-Holstein [State Government of Schleswig-Holstein] 2003).

Saxony-Anhalt introduced health targets in 1998 (Ministerium für Arbeit Frauen Gesundheit und Soziales des Landes Sachsen-Anhalt [Ministry for Work Women Health and Social Affairs of Saxony-Anhalt] 1998), renewed in 2004 (Ministerium für Gesundheit und Soziales Sachsen Anhalt [Ministry for Health and Social Affairs of Saxony-Anhalt] 2004) .

Baden-Württemberg: introduced targets in 2002 (Ministerium für Ernährung und Ländlichen Raum Baden-Württemberg [Ministry for Food and Rural Affairs Baden-Württemberg] 2002).

Lower Saxony: introduced targets in 2002 (Altgeld et al. 2004).

Mecklenburg-Western Pomerania: introduced targets in 2003 (2003).

Saxony: introduced targets in 2004 (Ministerium für Gesundheit und Soziales Sachsen Anhalt [Ministry for Health and Social Affairs of Saxony-Anhalt] 2004)(Ministerium für Gesundheit und Soziales Sachsen Anhalt 2004).

Brandenburg: adheres to a target-based process without formalized targets (von Braunmühl 2005).

Some German municipalities have also defined health targets. However, apart from municipalities like Bielefeld (Petzold 2005), renowned as a model of new public management, documentation is poor. Sickness funds have also defined health targets. The largest sickness fund, the Allgemeine Ortskrankenkassen (AOK), employed health targets as a tool to position itself in the market and the policy arena and currently the Federal Associations of the sickness funds have started another initiative to establish joint prevention targets.

As noted above, some activities in the health-care sector have features resembling those in health target programmes. The first DMP was introduced in February 2003 and focuses on diabetes. Other DMPs on breast cancer, asthma/chronic obstructive pulmonary disease (COPD) and cardiovascular disease have followed (Busse 2004).

The multitude of target initiatives in Germany reflects the diversity of influences that have contributed to their emergence. Among the most important is WHO's Health for All framework (WHO Regional Office for Europe 1999; WHO Regional Office for Europe 1985). The launch of the first federal initiative was a reaction to the adoption of the European Health for All policy in 1980 and, specifically, the publication of the targets in 1984. The minister then responsible for health (but not social health insurance) coined the phrase "cost-containment is not enough", suggesting that a comprehensive policy based on vision and values was indispensable. By the time health target setting became more common in Germany, the influence of

Health For All was diminishing. It played only a minor role in the second federal initiative.

Some contextual factors have prepared the ground for setting health targets. The emergence of health targets in Germany coincides with growing criticism of capacity planning and an interest in outcome-oriented reimbursement. This entails the specification of what can count as a desirable outcome. Effectively, this may result in target setting for individual patients, provider units or programmes. Similarly, an outcome has to be defined if the intention is to raise efficiency.

Less direct, but equally important, is the cultural change characterized by the widespread adoption of new public management. This has changed the perception of benchmarks and outcomes within state administrations. Another factor is the changing education of public health professionals. Postgraduate public health programmes were established in Germany only at the end of the 1980s. Previously, practitioners had to obtain Masters degrees in public health at foreign universities. In the United States of America they came into contact with the Healthy People programme (McGinnis 1985) which employs health targets.

Other contextual factors have hindered the emergence of health targets. First, German politics were somewhat polarized when health targets emerged – they were deemed a socialist instrument. This opened up an ideological schism between the two major political parties. The Social Democrats were in favour of targets, the Christian Democrats opposed them. Gradually, this schism has closed. Today the physicians' association and the physicians' chamber are promoters of health targets. Second, initially targets were opposed strongly by physicians who were against this interference with their statutory right to organize and manage service provision. Also, the sickness funds had little appetite for involvement with service provision. Gradually, this disagreement was overcome and the physicians' association changed its standpoint (Wismar and Busse 2000). Third, target setting in Germany had to take account of the vertical and horizontal fragmentation of political institutions. Responsibilities for health sit at different political levels. Social health insurance is regulated at the federal level while most public health services are regulated at the regional or local level. However, there are marked differences in institutional settings even between the regions (Wismar and Brasseit 2002). Within the insurance sector, health is not covered solely by the sickness funds. Accident insurance, pension insurance and other smaller programmes play important roles in prevention and rehabilitation and in general health care (Wismar et al. 2002). Finally, Germany's large substitutive private health insurance market also poses challenges.

Implementing health targets

Very little is known about the extent to which targets have contributed to health gain (Wismar 2003). There is evidence that health targets have supported better governance, with improved coordination within and between political levels, and contributed to policy innovations such as those on tobacco control.

Given that some of the regional health target initiatives started only in the early and mid 1990s, the absence of any form of systematic knowledge reflects the limited efforts to implement interventions as well as weaknesses in the health intelligence infrastructure. However, the picture is different for DMPs. Initial reports seem to suggest that diabetes outcomes have improved in the population enrolled in the programmes, but robust evaluation is not yet available since they were introduced only recently. Evidence on outcomes such as prevention of retinopathy and foot amputations will require longer follow-up (Kolpatzik and Meyers-Middendorf 2005).

Many providers conduct listed activities in support of the health targets. While this shows interest in the federal targets, it is of limited value as the list does not distinguish whether the activities were conducted before or after the introduction of the national health targets.

Another indicator of successful implementation might be the extent of citizens' knowledge of health targets. Yet very little is known about this. A representative telephone survey conducted by the Institute of Public Health in North Rhine-Westphalia showed that citizens themselves were able to formulate a consistent set of health priorities but were completely unaware of the ten targets set by the authorities (Boschek and Kügler 2002).

Target setting

Several approaches were used to select health targets or target topics in the various initiatives in Germany.

North Rhine-Westphalia used selection by example by selecting ten targets from those of the WHO European Region (Brasseit and Wismar 2002). Similarly, some of the Länder have decided to adopt health targets formulated within the framework of the federal initiative – gesundheitsziele.de. The rationale was to link the various levels of policy formulation and target definition in order to allow for a more concerted and effective approach covering different institutional levels (Altgeld 2005).

Schleswig-Holstein used selection by benchmarking – selecting targets for children's health, an area in which it lagged behind the German average.

A third method of selection was criteria driven. Criteria such as burden of disease and amenability to intervention were employed to screen conditions systematically and prioritize topics for target definition. This approach has been used extensively in the gesundheitsziele.de and the DMP.

A fourth was political relevance. Some critics did not consider breast cancer the most obvious choice for a DMP. However, political considerations influenced the decision-making process. To ensure consistency, breast cancer was then selected as a topic for the gesundheitsziele.de. However, the political approach is not necessarily devoid of criteria or unscientific. In Schleswig-Holstein a comparison of national data on the burden of disease was used to identify areas which were below average.

Whatever approach is used, there is a clear move towards involving stakeholders in the target-setting process. Some of the earlier initiatives (such as the first federal target-setting process or the targets developed in Hamburg) were defined by a small number of experts. This isolated approach is now seen as a major reason for the relatively low influence, or even failure, of these initiatives. Now stakeholders are involved in the processes to define and adopt targets there are problems with deciding which stakeholders should be involved and who is entitled to make the decision. The DMPs predefined stakeholders in the legal framework. Stakeholder participation in gesundheitsziele.de was managed by the project leader and the steering committee. This reflected the wide variety of issues covered – 200 experts, policy-makers and representatives from approximately 70 institutions took part. Representatives from patient and citizen groups were involved and had a strong influence on the work of all its committees and working groups (Gesellschaft für Versicherungswissenschaft und -gestaltung (GVG) e.V 2003).However, there has been no direct participation by patients and citizens and this has not been reported in any other health target initiative.

While target initiatives that did not involve stakeholders were facing problems of ownership and acceptability, stakeholder involvement did not necessarily ensure lasting support. Some of the participating organizations were sceptical observers; others took part in the process to fend off unwanted initiatives or remained inactive when the government failed to show decisive support.

Exerting influence

Governments, and other actors, can do much to ensure successful definition and implementation of health targets. Four different mechanisms will be reviewed: promotion, coordination, regulation and financial incentives.

Policy initiatives are often promoted with vigour and determination by the relevant ministries and their staff. In contrast, health targets have attracted rather less enthusiasm and generated little parliamentary debate. Not all health targets receive the blessing of other ministries or the Cabinet. For example, a proposed Cabinet endorsement of gesundheitsziele.de was denied because it contained rigorous tobacco control policy targets. Promotion of health targets is subject to changing priorities. These may reflect the appointment of a new minister (even if from the same coalition) or changing parliamentary majorities that may erode support. The strongest promotion of health targets often comes from the public health community.

Coordination is essential. Three major coordination efforts took place around the gesundheitsziele.de. The first sought to coordinate target definition at regional and federal levels. After the failure of the first federal initiative, the Länder became the driving force in defining health targets. They used the formal mechanism of the Health Ministers Conference (a biennial meeting of all Länder health ministers and the Federal Minister) to urge the federal government to define national health targets that would complement activities at the regional level. The conference adopted a resolution urging the Federal Ministry to define health targets (Gesundheitsministerkonferenz [Health ministers' conference] 1999). The ministers renewed their commitment by addressing a new resolution in 2006. This was a very important move as the audience was not just the Federal Ministry. This process has been observed closely by all stakeholders and interpreted as demonstrating an emergent national political will to take targets seriously. The Länder participated in the definition of the federal health targets through the group of chief medical officers and heads of relevant ministerial units.

Coordination can be seen in efforts to link health targets and DMPs. These initiatives were developed almost in parallel and all relevant stakeholders engaged with the DMP policy were also involved with health targets. The Federal Ministry of Health exerted political influence to ensure that at least diabetes and breast cancer were covered in gesundheitsziele.de. These were accepted after intense discussions but there was continuing controversy about the scope of health targets. Some stakeholders involved in the definition of DMPs were worried about the consequences of the health target process. They insisted that the health-care related aspects of diabetes and breast cancer should be excluded from the target-setting process in gesundheitsziele.de and addressed only in the DMPs. Other stakeholders felt that this would limit the scope for developing a comprehensive health policy, as the DMPs do not cover all aspects of these conditions. In essence, a conflict between these stakeholder groups spilled over into the health target policy arena.

The importance of coordination is apparent in the interaction between gesundheitsziele.de and the Prevention Forum (Forum Prävention). Initially, the new minister established a round table with associated working groups in order to establish consensus on future health-policy reform. However, it soon became clear that this was failing to reach consensus and all but one of the working groups ceased. The exception was health promotion and prevention. Supported by the minister, this working group developed into the Prevention Forum and planned a series of programmes and projects. There was considerable overlap of membership and topics between the Prevention Forum and gesundheitsziele.de. This caused practical problems and led to conflict between these two initiatives because not all organizations could follow both processes closely. It was not clear which initiative should have the lead in what field and there were anxieties about the allocation of scarce resources to finance the initiatives. This conflict had its repercussions inside the ministries since different units were responsible for different initiatives. It took a while to resolve this conflict by developing agreed structures to link the Ministry and the two initiatives.

By and large, health targets in Germany have not been associated with new regulations. One exception is the Public Health Service Act of Schleswig-Holstein which entered into force in 2001. This requires the formulation of health targets and obliges municipalities to take account of them.

At the federal level, the Prevention Act seemed to herald a breakthrough. In order to modernize health promotion and prevention, the Federal Ministry of Health was planning to introduce a new act establishing a prevention foundation. This would be a new mechanism to collect, pool and allocate existing funds dedicated to health promotion and prevention. It aimed to use this money more efficiently and more transparently in order to avoid overlaps, gaps and low-quality programmes and projects. The bill proposed that the allocation of funds should follow the priorities of the health targets set out by gesundheitsziele.de. Some criticized the alleged bureaucracy of the proposed foundation; some argued that it was unconstitutional to spend money on health promotion and prevention. The bill was not presented to Parliament and the 2005 general election meant that all deadlines were missed. A new, much more limited proposal for legislation was tabled in 2007. Health targets remained part of this.

The Ministry of Health has provided funding for the federal health targets initiative since December 2000. Federal funding for the management and coordination of all activities ceased in 2007 and was replaced by funding of single activities. Today the management and coordination of gesundheitsziele.de is financed by the health and pension insurance funds; physicians and hospital organizations; and manufacturers of medical products and pharmaceuticals. Originally it was planned that additional funding would be provided to integrate the initiative with the federal health reporting system organized by the Robert Koch Institute. The Ministry had announced further funding for beacon projects but budgetary constraints meant that these plans never matured. In principle, it was assumed that existing stakeholders would contribute to the implementation of gesundheitsziele.de by refocusing their activities. However, there was little incentive to do so as there was no advantage to anyone moving first. It was also unclear whether it was legal for social insurances to shift funds towards activities that contribute to the achievement of health targets.

Overall, there have been considerable efforts to coordinate the process of health targets, despite the previously mentioned ambiguous support of some key stakeholders. Yet, stable finance and regulation are missing. The experience with DMPs is completely different and shows how things can work. The Ministry of Health exerted considerable influence – setting extremely tight deadlines and threatening the self-governing actors (sickness funds, physicians' and hospital associations) with regulation without their consent. New regulations were introduced to amend the Social Code Book and financial incentives were created to encourage sickness funds to enrol chronically ill patients in DMPs.

Collecting and providing intelligence

There is clear evidence that health targets support the development of new health-intelligence activities. In most cases, the formulation of health targets requires a fresh approach to health intelligence. Often, the implementation of health targets requires previously unrecorded information.

In many cases, health targets emerged from an analysis of the existing situation – in Lower Saxony a regional report on the health of children and adolescents created a shared perception of the need to act. Similarly, the regional health targets in Hamburg, Schleswig-Holstein and Baden-Württemberg arose from regional assessments. The health targets in North Rhine-Westphalia are an exception as all ten were selected from the WHO Health for All targets. However, North Rhine-Westphalia produced health reports in 1990 and 1994, prior to the adoption of these health targets, (Ministerium für Gesundheit Soziales Frauen und Familie des Landes NRW [Ministry for Work Social Affairs and Health of North Rhine-Westphalia] 2005).

Epidemiological evidence is not sufficient for formulating health targets. Societal consensus is also required. This was achieved on the DMPs by the influential report of the Advisory Council for Concerted Action in Health Care. The report looked at the efficiency and adequacy of care and identified areas of over-, under- and mal-provision of services. It was based on a survey of all major health-care stakeholders, including payers, providers, self-help groups and government agencies (Sachverständigenrat für die Konzertierte Aktion im Gesundheitswesen [Advisory Council on the Assessment of Developments in the Health Care System] 2001). This report has been instrumental in defining not only the DMPs but also the targets in gesundheitsziele.de.

In many cases, the process of implementing health targets has supported the development of health reporting. North Rhine-Westphalia provides an important example that impacted on other Länder. One of the ten targets adopted in 1995 focused on health intelligence – by 2005, a health information system should support the definition, implementation, monitoring and evaluation of the Health for All policy. As a result, both regional- and local-level health reporting in North Rhine-Westphalia was codified by the new Public Health Service Act in 1998. Since then a regional set of more than 300 indicators and a local (district-level) set of more than 50 indicators have become available. In 2003, under the leadership of North Rhine-Westphalia, all German Länder agreed on a revised regional set of indicators. Alongside this process, special health reports focusing on gender; migration; children and adolescents; and health and illness were published and a health portal was established (Ministerium für Gesundheit Soziales Frauen und Familie des Landes NRW 2005). At the federal level, the Robert Koch Institute sought to link the topics of the reports with the targets in gesundheitsziele.de (Horch and Ziese 2005).

Yet, despite these numerous developments, health intelligence is not adequate to evaluate the health targets. Even in North Rhine-Westphalia, the evaluation of progress towards health targets conceded that the health-intelligence infrastructure did not allow full assessment (Ministerium für Gesundheit Soziales Frauen und Familie des Landes NRW 2005). This problem was envisaged when gesundheitsziele.de was planned, but was considered primarily due to insufficient evidence on policies and interventions rather lack of epidemiological data. It was not clear which organizations were to conduct what intervention and how.

REFERENCES

Altgeld T (2005). Gesundheitsziele für Kinder und Jugendliche auf Bundes-, Landes- und kommunaler ebene. In: Gesellschaft für Versicherungswissenschaft und -gestaltung (GVG) e.V *gesundheitsziele.de: Impulse, Wirkungen und Erfahrungen.* Berlin, Akademische Verlagsgesellschaft AKA:67-77.

Altgeld T et al. (2004). *Dokumentation der Gesundheitszielkonferenz für Niedersachsen 2003.* Hanover, Niedersächsisches Ministerium für Soziales, Frauen, Familie und Gesundheit.

Behörde für Arbeit Gesundheit und Soziales Freie und Hansestadt Hamburg (1995). *Gesundheit von Kindern und Jugendlichen in Hamburg - Zwischenbilanz 1994.* Hamburg.

Behörde für Arbeit Gesundheit und Soziales Freie und Hansestadt Hamburg (1992). *Stadtdiagnose.* Hamburg.

Boschek H-J, Kügler KJ (2002). Communal health targets as seen by the population and by experts. Two inquiries in the Ennepe-Ruhr District. *Gesundheitswesen,* 64:633-638.

Brasseit U, Wismar M (2002). Inhaltliche Ausrichtung und konkrete Themen - Zielkorb zur exemplarischen Auswahl für gesundheitsziele.de In: Gesellschaft für Versicherungswissenschaft und -gestaltung (GVG) e.V *Gesundheitsziele.de - Forum Gesundheitsziele für Deutschland. Entwicklung, Ausrichtung, Konzepte.* Köln, Akademische Verlagsgesellschaft AKA GmbH:71-100.

Bundesministerium für Gesundheit (2007). *Erster Arbeitsentwurf eines Gesetzes zur Stärkung der Gesundheitsförderung und gesundheitlicher Prävention sowie zur Änderung anderer Gesetze.* Berlin, Federal Ministry of Health.

Busse R (2004). Disease management programs in Germany's statutory health insurance system. *Health Affairs,* 23(3):56-67.

Gesellschaft für Versicherungswissenschaft und Gestaltung (GVG) e.V (2003). *gesundheitsziele.de - Forum zur Entwicklung und Umsetzung von Gesundheitszielen in Deutschland.* Berlin, Federal Ministry of Health and Social Security.

Horch K, Ziese T (2005). Das Zusammenspiel von Gesundheitsberichterstattung und Gesundheitszielen In: *Gesellschaft für Versicherungswissenschaft und -gestaltung (GVG) e.V* Berlin, Akademische Verlagsgesellschaft AKA:245-250.

Joos S et al. (2005). ELSID-Diabetes study – evaluation of a large scale implementation of disease management programmes for patients with type 2 diabetes. Rationale, design and conduct – a study protocol. *BMC Public Health,* 5:99.

Klus H., Angele S, Mennicken R (2007). Ziele auf Bundesebene. In: *Gesellschaft für Versicherungswissenschaft und -gestaltung (GVG) e.V. Gesundheitsziele im Föderalismus: Programme der Länder und des Bundes.* Bonn, Nanos Verlag oHG.

Kolpatzik K, Meyers-Middendorf J (2005). Zielführende Maßnahmen der GKV im Bereich der krankheitsbezogenen Ziele: das Disease Management Programe zum Diabetes Typ 2. In: e. Gesellschaft für Versicherungswissenschaft und -gestaltung (GVG) e.V. *Gesundheitsziele.de: Impulse, Wirkungen und Erfahrungen.* Berlin, Akademische Verlagsgesellschaft AKA:163-169.

Landesregierung Schleswig-Holstein (2003). *Gesundheitsziele für Schleswig-Holstein* (http://landesregierung.schleswig-holstein.de/coremedia/generator/Aktueller20Bestand/ MSGV/Information/Gesundheitsziele.html, accessed 1 August 2008).

McGinnis JM (1985). Setting nationwide objectives in disease prevention and health promotion: the United States experience. In: Holland WW, Detels S, Knox G, eds. *Oxford textbook of public health. Investigative methods in public health.* Oxford, Oxford University Press.

Ministerium für Arbeit Frauen Gesundheit und Soziales des Landes Sachsen-Anhalt (1998). *Gesundheitliche Lage der Bevölkerung in Sachsen-Anhalt und Ableitung von Gesundheitszielen für das Land. Dokumentation der 1. Landesgesundheitskonferenz vom 26. März 1998.* Magdeburg, Ministry for Work, Women, Health and Social Affairs of Saxony-Anhalt.

Ministerium für Arbeit, Gesundheit und Soziales (1999) *Ziele für die Gesundheitspolitik - Antrag Nordrhein-Westfalen- Gesundheitsministerkonferenz Trier, 9-10 June 1999.*

Ministerium für Arbeit Gesundheit und Soziales des Landes Schleswig-Holstein (1997). *Zur Gesundheitslage der Kinder in Schleswig-Holstein: Daten, Einschätzungen, Fragen.* Kiel, Ministry for Work, Health and Social Affairs of Schleswig-Holstein.

Ministerium für Arbeit Soziales und Gesundheit des Landes Nordrhein-Westfalen (1995). *Zehn vorrangige gesundheitsziele für NRW.* Bielefeld, Landesinstitut für den ÖGD des Landes NRW.

Ministerium für Ernährung und Ländlichen Raum Baden-Württemberg (2002). *Kinderernährung in Baden-Württemberg.* Baden-Baden, Ministry for Food and Rural Affairs Baden-Württemberg.

Ministerium für Gesundheit Soziales Frauen und Familie des Landes NRW (2005). *Gesundheitsziele NRW 2005-2010. Grundlagen für die nordrhein-westfälische Gesundheitspolitik.* Bielefeld, Ministry for Work, Social Affairs and Health of North Rhine-Westphalia]

Ministerium für Gesundheit und Soziales Sachsen Anhalt (2004). *Künftig fünf gesundheitsziele für Sachsen-Anhalt. Minister Kley: gesundheitsförderung und prävention stärken, gesundheitskompetenz des einzelnen* (http://www.sachsen-anhalt.de/rcs/LSA/pub/Ch1/fld8311011390180834/mainfldyzhadi3ac7/fldqttfbnbbfc/pgf6t1c6j2lz/index.jsp, accessed 1 August 2008.

Petzold C (2005). Die Arbeit mit Gesundheitszielen auf kommunaler Ebene - das Beispiel der Stadt Bielefeld In: Gesellschaft für Versicherungswissenschaft und -gestaltung (GVG) e.V *Gesundheitsziele.de. Impulse, Wirkungen und Erfahrungen.* Berlin, Akademische Verlagsgesellschaft AKA:89-96.

Sachverständigenrat für die Konzertierte Aktion im Gesundheitswesen (2001). *Bedarfsgerechtigkeit und wirtschaftlichkeit. Band III: Über-, Unter- und Fehlversorgung. Gutachten 2000/2001. Ausführliche Zusammenfassung.* Advisory Council on the Assessment of Developments in the Health Care System (http://www.svrgesundheit.de/Gutachten/Gutacht01/kurzf-engl01.pdf, accessed 1 August 2008).

von Braunmühl C (2005). Die Entwickung von Gesundheitszielen in Brandenburg. In: Gesellschaft für Versicherungswissenschaft und -gestaltung (GVG) e.V. *Gesundheitsziele.de: Impulse, Wirkungen und Erfahrungen.* Berlin, Akademische Verlagsgesellschaft AKA: 79-88.

Weber I. et al. (1990). *Dringliche Gesundheitsprobleme der Bevölkerung in der Bundesrepublik Deutschland: Zahlen - Fakten - Perspektiven.* Baden-Baden, Nomos Verlagsgesellschaft.

Weber I, Meye MR, Flatten G (1987). *Vorrangige Gesundheitsprobleme in den verschiedenen Lebensabschnitten: Zwischenbericht.* Baden-Baden, Nomos Verlagsgesellschaft.

Wismar M (2003). Gesundheitsziele in internationaler Perspektive. *Bundesgesundheitsblatt,* 46(2):105-108.

Wismar M, Brasseit U (2002). Gesundheitsziele im Mehrebenensystem. In: Gesellschaft für versicherungswissenschaft und -gestaltung (GVG) e.V. *Gesundheitsziele.de - Forum Gesundheitsziele für Deutschland. Gesundheitsziele für Deutschland: Entwicklung, Ausrichtung, Konzepte.* Köln, Akademische Verlagsgesellschaft AKA GmbH:113-148.

Wismar M, Brasseit U, Angele S (2002). Multisektorale Ausrichtung von Gesundheitszielen. In: Gesellschaft für versicherungswissenschaft und -gestaltung (GVG) e.V Gesundheitsziele.de - Forum Gesundheitsziele für Deutschland *Gesundheitsziele für Deutschland: Entwicklung,*

Ausrichtung, Konzepte. Köln, Akademische Verlagsgesellschaft AKA GmbH:39-50.

Wismar M, Busse R (2000). Targets for health in Germany. *European Journal of Public Health,* 10(4):38-42.

WHO Regional Office for Europe (1999). *Health21: the Health for All policy framework for the WHO European Region.* Copenhagen, WHO Regional Office for Europe.

WHO Regional Office for Europe (1985). *Targets for Health for All. Targets in support of the European regional strategy for health for all.* Copenhagen, WHO Regional Office for Europe.

Chapter 10

Hungary: Targets Driving Improved Health Intelligence

Zoltán Vokó, Róza Ádány

Historical overview

Target-based public health policy-making in Hungary is over ten years old. Previous Hungarian health policies had covered almost exclusively the administrative, financial and legal aspects of health services. The WHO Health for All policy placed the health status of the population at the centre of health policy-making in Hungary.

Priorities of Public Health until the Millennium was the first comprehensive health programme in Hungary to use the health target setting method. Initiated by the chief medical officer and based on an analysis of the burden of diseases and of health determinants, it defined 5 national goals to be achieved by 2000, 10 national tasks and 20 programmes. Although issued as a government decree (in 1994) that came into force in January 1995, the programme was never launched because of a lack of political and financial support. The reasons for political disregard were complex. Firstly, the programme was developed by a small group of experts so important stakeholders did not see it as their own initiative. Secondly, at that time few people in the health administration thought that their responsibility lay beyond the borders of health-service provision. Thirdly, health was not high on the political agenda in Hungary's transitional society of the mid 1990s when severe economical, structural and social problems were seen as the priorities.

The next major step in target-based health policy-making was the For the Healthy Nation national public health programme set out in a government decree in 2001. This followed the structure of the previous programme by setting national goals, tasks and subprogrammes to be achieved over ten years, but with a wider scope and updated content. Only the nationwide mammography screening programme came into effect during the period of the government that launched the programme. The new government undertook to continue the programme in a slightly modified format as the Johan Béla National Programme for the Decade of Health. In 2003, this gained almost unanimous parliamentary approval for the period from 2003 to 2012 (Parliament of the Republic of Hungary 2003).

Development of the policies

The policies described above were initiated by public health professionals who realized that existing health service oriented policies, could not respond to the challenge posed by the very unfavourable health status of the Hungarian population. In the late 1990s, for example, health professionals worked with MSD Hungary Inc. to develop the target-based Sound Heart programme. This was an ambitious cardiovascular preventive programme consisting of health-promotion activities; primary and secondary prevention programmes for hypertension and diabetes mellitus; improvements in cardiovascular diagnostic, curative and rehabilitation services; training programmes for professionals; and the development of monitoring for cardiovascular diseases. Although well-received by the administration, it never acquired formal legal status and was not implemented. Later, elements were incorporated in the national public health programme.

In November 2000, the medical section of the Hungarian Academy of Sciences invited representatives of public health professionals and health policy-makers to a Science Speaks to Policy forum at which the necessity of a comprehensive national public health programme was emphasized and accepted by all parties. This event had a great impact on the development of the For the Healthy Nation programme. This (and the subsequent programme) was heavily influenced by international examples, primarily WHO's Health for All strategy and national programmes from the United Kingdom.

Hungarian target-based public health programmes expanded beyond the borders of health policy at that time. They aimed to implement modern, intersectoral, multidisciplinary public health actions. While recognizing government responsibility, there was an emphasis on the involvement of civil society, local authorities, the private sector and the general public.

As the new public health approach became dominant in international health policy discourse (such as the public health programmes of the EU) and the need to improve the health of the population became a more visible political issue in Hungary, the health administration accepted its broader responsibility.

In the 1990s, the World Bank supported a programme aimed at reforming public health services and training in Hungary that contributed much to the transformation of the health administration. In 1999 a public health department was established in the Ministry of Health. Subsequently, professional initiatives were backed by political support from the health administration.

For the Healthy Nation was the first public health programme to achieve the legal status of a government decree. This legal underpinning was in line with the multisectoral approach of the programme. Its sustainability was emphasized when it was continued by parliamentary decree in 2003. These programmes defined tasks for a range of actors and sectors but policy-makers and other actors outside the health sector were rarely involved in their development. In 2002 an interministerial committee was established to coordinate them but could not fulfil its role because it lacked an appropriate financing mechanism. The national public health programme was allocated a separate, very limited, budget line but later even this was decreased year by year. Screening programmes; communication campaigns; and community and human resource development programmes have been financed from this resource but the programme managers had no formal means by which to influence the policies and budgets of other sectors, such as education, agriculture or taxation. Since health is not a priority in most of these sectors, their administrations were (and are) reluctant to accept any health-sector influence on their policies.

Furthermore, beyond the health administration the new public health approach was accepted only slowly within the health sector itself. Public health programmes have not yet been integrated with other health policies. This slow acceptance in health services (such as the primary-care sector) is mostly due to a lack of knowledge and skills among the health professionals concerned. Hence, there was a key development when a Faculty of Public Health was created at the University of Debrecen. This brought together the Departments of Preventive Medicine, Behavioural Sciences and Family Care and offers the potential for a greater acceptance of new concepts and public health tasks within the health service. This new collaboration allowed training in hygiene to be geared towards modern preventive medicine and public health by means of enhanced courses for medical students; residency programmes in preventive medicine and public health; and the launch of a family medicine programme.

Nevertheless, as in many other countries, Hungary's key health-policy issues remain the finance and management of health services. Most such policies are developed separately from public health considerations thus impairing the efficiency of policy-making and creating inconsistencies in implementation.

Defining health targets

The scope of the programmes increased gradually between 1994 and 2003. The latest programme covers major health issues; the socioeconomical, environmental and behavioural determinants of health; health of designated age groups; health inequalities; different settings for health promotion; and the necessary human and institutional development for implementation. Some of these targets are listed in Box 10-1.

Box 10-1 *Selected targets of the Johan Béla National Programme for the Decade of Health*

Life expectancy at birth should increase by three years for both genders in a perspective of ten years [was 68.4 years for men; 76.8 for women in 2003].

Improvements in the morbidity and mortality rates of socially excluded population groups (within ten years).

Improved opportunities for socially excluded population groups to access equal and discrimination-free health-care services – within three years [of those who used health services, 35% of persons living in Roma settlements suffered discrimination in 2004].

Reduce the prevalence of regular smoking by 6% (to about 35% among males) by 2010 [42% smokers among men in 2003].

Number of alcohol abusers, binge drinkers and problem drinkers will decline and by 2012 the estimated number of alcoholics will be fewer than 500 000 [3% of women (~130 000) and 18% of men (~ 680 000) were heavy drinkers in 2003].

Consumption of fruit and vegetables will rise from the current 300 grams/day to 400-450 grams/day.

Cut premature mortality due to coronary heart and cerebrovascular diseases by 20% [standardized (European old standard population) death rate due to cardiovascular diseases at age 0-64 years 121.5/100 000 in 2003].

Stop the rising mortality trends due to tumours.

Prevent new HIV infection, maintain a low incidence of infection, reduce AIDS morbidity by 20% and mortality by 25% in ten years [0.62 /100 000 new reported HIV infections in 2003].

Have 70% of women between the ages of 45-65 participate in mammography screening repeated biennially [~ 60% in 2003].

Expand the sphere of primary health-care activity by introducing lifestyle counselling.

Quantitative targets were defined in all areas, primarily as a means of monitoring the programme. The Hungarian health-monitoring system was unable to provide nationwide information on the targets until 2003. Most of the targets failed to take account of the huge social and geographical inequalities in health and the actual values of the targets were heavily criticized by professionals. However, with no tradition of public health forecasting in Hungary, it is questionable whether more valid targets could have been developed in the short run.

On the other hand, the programme itself boosted health monitoring. Traditionally, different health-monitoring activities were the responsibility of different institutions. For example, mortality registration is run by the Central Statistical Office (HCSO); notification of communicable diseases is managed by the National Public Health and Medical Officer Service. Only aggregated data are published annually in the HCSO's statistical yearbooks. Before the late 1990s, there was little coordination between the different institutions. The content of the health statistics system was reviewed regularly from the statistical point of view but the actual needs of health policy-making and evaluation did not play an important role in the development of the system. Also, the end products of the monitoring system were mostly aggregated data that could not be translated easily into the information formats needed for policy purposes.

The target-based nature of the public health programmes, and the need to monitor their processes, outputs and outcomes, necessitated the development of a health-monitoring system. This was supported by the EU health monitoring programme (McKee and Ryan 2003). Regular state-of-the-art health surveys (Johan Béla National Centre for Epidemiology 2003); a novel sentinel surveillance programme involving general practitioners (Szeles et al. 2005); and new forms of public health reporting have been incorporated into the monitoring system (Johan Béla National Centre for Epidemiology 2003a). The government is required to report to parliament on the implementation of the programme every year and on progress towards the targets every four years (Johan Béla National Centre for Epidemiology 2003b). An annual forum on health statistics enhances cooperation between the institutions responsible for health monitoring.

The recognition of significant inequalities in health among different regions of Hungary (Ádány 2003; Kósa et al. 2007) revealed the need for a countrywide network of regional health observatories that can monitor trends and patterns of health and health determinants; identify gaps in information and services; highlight future problems; assess the health impact of programmes and policies; and disseminate information to policy-makers and other users (McKee et al. 2004).

The first regional health observatory (throughout central and eastern Europe) was established in the north-east Hungary twin-region (total population: 2.9 million). Starting at the end of 2005, it employs geographical information systems to collect and analyse a wide range of demographic and epidemiological data. These are linked to data on the provision of services in order to produce relevant data that can support health policy-makers. Importantly, it impacts on the policy agenda by highlighting patterns and trends that had been invisible. Looking ahead, the National Development Plan 2007–2013 envisages the extension of this network throughout the country as a key element of the future development of public health services. However, the small number of appropriately trained public health professionals is a major barrier for further progress (Adany et al. 2002).

Implementation (including intended and unintended effects) and monitoring

Only the latest programme is being implemented on a reasonable scale. The implementation activities could be divided into two groups (Ministry of Health Budapest 2004). First, non-health sector activities were managed and supervised by the appropriate ministries. Each continued with their usual activities but submitted their plans and reports to the national Interministerial Committee of Public Health, chaired by the governmental Public Health Commissioner. Collaboration between the different sectors remained ad hoc and partial. However, there are good examples of collaboration. The National Environmental Health Action Plan (a subprogramme of the public health programme) was developed and implemented with the environment and health ministries. One successful shared project was a survey of buildings containing asbestos; another developed an aerobiological network. The education and health ministries work together to improve health education in schools. This collaboration introduced the concept of the health-promoting school within the updated version of the law on public education. This required all elementary schools to develop and execute a health-promotion plan. The number of gymnastics classes increased and a ministerial decree was issued concerning standards in school canteens. The government subsidized the development of a health education and health promotion curriculum, with accompanying teaching material, to be incorporated into basic teacher training.

The second group of activities is the responsibility of the health administration. This includes legislative tasks, screening programmes and competitions for funding for healthy settlement and healthy workplace projects, school health projects, communication campaigns, etc. Competition for local projects catalysed initiatives by communities and workplaces. Monitoring and evaluation of the projects fed back into continued development of the competitions. For example, the competition for healthy workplaces was split into two parts following the evaluation of the projects from 2003. In one call for proposals, workplaces could apply for funding to implement the development and execution of their health-promotion programmes. Most applications were received from public institutions and small enterprises which had no existing health-promoting activities and lacked the necessary resources to start them. In the second call for proposals, workplaces could apply for the official title of Health Promoting Workplace. This rewarded their activities and results and gave moral support for continuous development.

The institutional framework for the implementation of the programme is under continuous development. Unfortunately, the roles of the different actors have changed several times, thus slowing down implementation and frustrating the participants. The programme has not achieved widespread public participation because few professionals in the Public Health and Medical Officer Service and in the municipalities are trained in health promotion and capable of coordinating the different actors at local level; and there are inadequate financial resources.

Central programmes, such as cancer screening and mass media campaigns are implemented via the central administration together with the National Public Health and Medical Officer Service. Mammography and cervical screening programmes, based on registration and invitation, started in the framework of the public health programme. The screening programmes have developed an effective collaboration between the curative medical services and the National Public Health and Medical Officer Service. However, this collaboration is not without conflicts. For example, cervical screening could not be based in the primary health-care service because of active resistance from the gynaecologists who traditionally perform opportunistic screening.

The National Institute for Health Promotion is the key coordinator of the implementation of health promoting programmes and the responsible institute for process and output monitoring. Together with the Ministry of Health it engages with different partners to implement projects, as shown in the annual work plans. The National Centre for Epidemiology is responsible for monitoring targets, performing national health surveys and compiling the public health reports. Its main findings are included in the yearly reports to parliament that cover the health of the population. These began in 2004; a similar report at the mid-point of the public health programme (in 2008) may lead to updating of the targets.

Exerting influence

Health has become more and more of an issue on the political agenda in Hungary. On the political level, the health of the population and the reduction of health inequalities have been declared as priorities. Increasing interest in health from the public, nongovernmental organizations and the media has increasingly influenced this development. Within the public health programme, media campaigns not only raise public awareness and motivate action on health but also maintain pressure on policy-makers.

The very traditional view that health is an individual responsibility has been changing slowly. Many years spent promoting a new vision of health has resulted in a better acceptance of the role of social, behavioural and environmental determinants. This served as a basis to create multisectoral public health programmes that defined the responsibility of the different sectors and actors. The establishment of the national Interministerial Committee of Public Health reflects this development. The state actively promotes collaboration by different actors at local level, providing financial support for the development and implementation of local health plans involving different actors.

Yet, after ten years, there is still no legal (or other) pressure on the administration to develop target-based health policies. Only political will determines whether or not a health policy is target based. At the moment there is no formal infrastructure for health target setting, either centrally or locally.

Lessons learned

The Hungarian experience provides many lessons for others seeking to develop target-based health strategies.

Target-based public health policies offered a useful framework for planning and implementing actions in Hungary. Targets helped to make health policies objective, oriented and accountable; not only in terms of their implementation but also in outputs and outcomes. Nevertheless, targets can serve this purpose only if they are designed to be challenging but achievable. This requires more attention to the scientific basis of target setting – the process and responsibilities should be clear.

The establishment of a regional health observatory network in Hungary is a key element in taking health targets to the next stage. At present, the public health programme is too centralized, missing many opportunities arising from local initiatives. The importance of projects that respond to local problems will increase as decentralization of the administration continues and disaggregated health information becomes available at regional and community levels.

A multisectoral approach can be successful only if the different sectors are involved from the inception of the planning phase and if the centre coordinating the programme has the necessary administrative power. However, it is a difficult legal problem to create such a centre when ministers are fully accountable and responsible for different sectors. Horizontal coordinating bodies usually do not have the necessary power in the Hungarian public administration.

Long-term political support is essential. It can be difficult to provide the necessary financial support even if the public health programme has wide political backing. This situation is unlikely to change so innovative ways of fund raising from business partners and local authorities should be developed. Furthermore, legislation that creates financial incentives for the different actors should be used in a more systematic way. For example, by adjusting the financing of the work of primary care physicians to increase their involvement in prevention. The current income tax rules relating to expenses on health promoting and preventive services in the framework of private health insurance can be developed further to mobilize public resources.

The involvement of nongovernmental organizations, local authorities, private and academic sectors and the media is crucial for success. Strategic planning and implementation should be based on consensus building and partnership. However, the government does have a role in financing the national public health programme and should act as a catalyst through coordination and the provision of know-how.

Public participation can be achieved if local and central authorities support each other. Decentralization of activities helps with the outreach of the public health programme. People involved in local health education and health promotion projects are reached more easily by central programmes.

Human resource development is an essential part of any public health programme in Hungary. There is a need for professionalism in their planning, management and evaluation. Recent achievements demonstrate the value of the new public health training. Graduates of the MSc programmes from the School of Public Health at Debrecen actively contribute to planning, implementation and monitoring of the public health programme at both central and local level. However, their legal status is often ambiguous. There is a clear need for a formal recognition of public health professionals and the roles that they play.

REFERENCES

Ádány R (2003). *A magyar lakosság egészségi állapota az ezredfordulón (The health status of the Hungarian population at the turn of the millennium).* Budapest, Medicina.

Adany R et al. (2002). Public health challenges of the 21st century and the role of schools of public health in central and eastern Europe. *Public Health Review,* 30(1-4):15-33.

Johan Béla National Centre for Epidemiology (2003b). *Briefing for Parliament on progress made by Johan Béla National Programme for the Decade of Health in 2003..* Budapest, Johan Béla National Centre for Epidemiology.

Johan Béla National Centre for Epidemiology (2003). *National health interview survey 2003 Hungary - executive update.* Budapest, Johan Béla National Centre for Epidemiology (available at: http://www.oek.hu/oekfile.pl?fid=533, accessed 1 February 2006).

Johan Béla National Centre for Epidemiology (2003a). *National Public Health Update 2003,* Budapest, Johan Béla National Centre for Epidemiology (available at: http://www.oek.hu/oekfile.pl?fid=523, accessed 1 February 2006).

Kósa Z et al. (2007). Health of the inhabitants of Roma settlements in Hungary: a comparative health survey. *American Journal of Public Health,* 97(5):853-859.

McKee M, Ádány R, MacLehose L (2004). Health status and trends in candidate countries. In: McKee M, MacLehose L, Nolte E, eds. *Health policy and European enlargement.* Maidenhead, Open University Press: 24-42.

McKee M, Ryan J (2003). Monitoring health in Europe: opportunities, challenges and progress. *European Journal of Public Health,* 13(Suppl. 3):1-4.

Ministry of Health Budapest (2004). *National Public Health Programme Action Plan 2004.* Budapest, Ministry of Health.

Parliament of the Republic of Hungary (2003). *Johan Béla National Programme for the Decade of Health.* Budapest, Parliament of the Republic of Hungary.

Szeles G et al. (2005). A preliminary evaluation of a health monitoring programme in Hungary. *European Journal of Public Health* 15(1):26-32.

Chapter 11

The Russian Federation: Difficult History of Target Setting

Kirill Danishevski

Historical overview

Linguistic confusion complicates any description of the target-setting process in the Russian Federation. This is not only because certain words do not have an exact translation but also because the same word can mean slightly different things. Health policy is one term that creates confusion as politics and policy are the same word in the Russian language. The political environment during the Soviet period did not permit the emergence of what would generally be described as health policy. Even now, some discussions between international agencies and Russian government officials (supported by the best possible translation) have left both sides confused. Recently a number of senior officials in development organizations have begun to ask: what is health policy in the Russian Federation?

Policy documents in the form of Communist Party five-year plans, decrees, instructions at various levels and informal communications are used to formulate what would be called health policy elsewhere. Recently a number of strategic papers have emerged but their status is not clear and it is not known whether they form part of a health policy. Before 2003 there were some attempts to formulate a strategic vision of what kind of changes were needed in health care. The later emergence of Health, one of the National Priority Projects, diverged from a comprehensive approach to a set of narrowly focused targeted activities. Differences in language, mentality, history and the way the state works thus offer the potential to create confusion about the abstract phenomenon of a health policy. It is necessary to examine how the Russian state evolved during the twentieth century in order to understand the role of target setting.

The roots of target setting in the Russian Federation

As a management approach, target setting has a long history in the Russian Federation. The Soviet Union and other communist countries present a unique case where market forces were disregarded in all sectors of the economy. Central planning was the only alternative to the market which corresponded with the prevailing ideology. This involved defining objectives, implementing activities to achieve them, and then measuring how well they were achieved. No matter how small, every aspect of the economy had to be defined, quantified and monitored at some level in the system, with regulation from the very top. Within the Soviet Union, a far greater proportion of the economy was fully based on management by objectives than in virtually any other country.

However, the use of targets predates the Soviet period. Debate about the effectiveness of centralized rule (initially the monarchy) rather than a more democratic and market-oriented system dates back to the eighteenth century. The Zapadniki (westerners) who called for a more liberal, market-based system argued with Slavianofili (Slavic-oriented) members of the Russian elite, who viewed their country as part of neither Asia nor Europe. Slavianofili were convinced that central governance was required to guide Russians to happiness.

In 1864, a series of reforms affected the courts, military, university and financial sectors by limiting censorship and abolishing serfdom. They also created a system of local self-government based on districts (zemstvo) which established the basis of a health system based on district medical officers or general practitioners. The district (zemski) medical officer was responsible for a defined population and accountable to the zemstvo committee. Yet, despite this seemingly major devolution of power, the Russian Empire remained a centralized monarchy – the authorities in Moscow retained the right to intervene in any decisions made in the regions and districts.

Communist approach to target setting

Soviet communists perceived the market as something that would lead to inequity, exploitation of the working class and promotion of the interests of a rich minority. The positive effects of markets and the negative consequences of central planning were overlooked or neglected. The Communist Party was highly hierarchical and opposed to any alternative ways of thinking, it did not permit any diversion from the set goals. One of its functions was to define the goals that were considered to represent the interests of all Soviet people. The Central Committee of the Communist Party (a body of relatively few people) established goals and related targets for most areas of the economy.

The Communist Party plenums met once every five years to obtain formal approval for its five-year plan. These pyatiletka were primarily concerned with structures (such as the building of new roads, bridges, factories and hospitals) and objectives for international activities to help other, mainly postcolonial countries, fight for working-class rule. However, five-year plans seldom looked in any detail at how to increase the effectiveness of what already existed, or how to manage people or the infrastructure. Moreover, population health was simply not on the agenda once the major epidemics of communicable diseases confronting the new Soviet state had been dealt with.

The western concept of using health targets as a health policy tool derives from the management by objectives (MBO) approach developed in the middle of the twentieth century (Drucker 1954). This focused on outcomes rather than activity. Both during and after the Soviet period, the majority of targets in all fields (including health) until recently were process or even input oriented: for instance, building new facilities, training more physicians, etc. Some objectives were even broader and concerned with implementation of complex ideologies or systems at large. A goal to implement free medical care for all Soviet people was set soon after the revolution in 1917.

Effective implementation of a target-based strategy requires routine monitoring and a means of intervention if progress stalls. The Soviet system of planning might have been more effective if the communist ideology had permitted some notion of criticism, based on objective and independent evaluation and debate. Instead, the Party would not admit failure to reach the objectives it had set. In a few cases, where no other excuse was forthcoming, they blamed "enemies of the Soviet people" and often prosecuted people for sabotaging the process. This made targets effectively self-fulfilling. Although there were some real achievements in the first half of the twentieth century, creating the illusion of success became the default strategy where the system failed to achieve its objectives.

Motivating people to achieve targets was another issue. The Soviet government's official policy of promoting equality did not provide any opportunity to create positive incentives. Under Stalin the main motivation was negative as failure potentially led to the gulag, but this threat was reduced under Khrushchev. The lack of financial incentives was partially compensated for by a system of in-kind incentives. Being a member of the Communist Party could also offer toleration in cases of underperformance. Widespread informal payments further compromised the pursuit of government objectives, as individuals responded to these unofficial incentives.

Health and target setting

Historically, health was never a major priority in the Russian Federation. This reflected a political emphasis on economic and industrial development in the late nineteenth century; the wars and revolutions in the early twentieth century; and finally (according to Lenin's April Theses) placing the interests of the working class above those of society in general. This ideology led to a failure to value life and health, sacrificed for the goal of building communism. Indeed, the first Soviet leadership had commissars for education, telegraph, post-offices, railways and many other sectors but not for health. Health care receded further down the list of priorities after the Cuban Missile Crisis. Physicians' incomes were 80% of the national average in the Soviet Union, linked to the growing feminization of the medical workforce, of whom 80% were women (Field 1999). This indicates the higher priority given to heavy industry and the military rather than social well-being.

Health issues were tackled relatively effectively in the early years of the Soviet Union and between the end of the Second World War and the mid 1960s. In part this was because the Soviet Union gave a high priority to the control of infectious disease from the outset. Lenin famously stated that "if communism does not destroy the louse, the louse will destroy communism" (Field 1957). The main communicable diseases at that time required relatively simple interventions such as vaccination, quarantine, sanitation measures, sewage systems and clean water supplies. Considerable improvements in health were achieved but the objectives pursued related to structures and processes. Explicit outcomes were sought rarely, unless (for example) an epidemic occurred and eradication was possible.

The epidemiological transition (Omran 1971) led to a change in the health needs of the population in the mid 1960s. This coincided with the Soviet government's radical change of priorities that produced a significant decline in spending on health (Andreev et al. 2003). The government attempted to address the growth of noncommunicable diseases using the more-of-the-same approach at a time when expenditure on health was declining. This led to a situation where life expectancy actually began to fall (Tulchinsky and Varavikova 1996). However, rather than trying to redress this, the life-expectancy figures were suppressed in annual reports from the late 1960s until the end of the Soviet Union. Ideology and the leadership's inability to admit mistakes and search openly for solutions caused similar reactions in many other sectors.

The debate about the advantages and disadvantages of systems that are self-regulated or those with more central guidance continues to this day in the Russian Federation. There are ongoing discussions about the role of target setting as a health-care management tool. Given the extensive experience of using a complex set of targets and indicators in a vertical command system in the Soviet Union, the Russian Federation offers a good opportunity for exploring the impact of targets.

There is also an examination of attempts to change the system of health-care management through the 2005 introduction of performance-based funding and setting of health-care objectives based on outcome measures..

Implementation, intended and unintended outcomes

As noted, until recently, health was seldom prominent on the government's policy agenda and the concept of effectiveness was discussed little in relation to health. The reasons for this situation were primarily ideological. This section discusses the Russian experience with target setting and why it had such a limited impact on health-system reform.

Nonspecific targets

A mismatch between objectives announced and outcomes achieved was apparent even in the overall purposes of the Soviet health system. Free and egalitarian health care was a formal goal yet there were parallel systems for the bureaucratic elite and workers in certain industries and ministries. This provision of higher quality services to some groups in the population could not be publicized because it contradicted the major principles of the Soviet state. In practice, it was simply accepted and even considered fair that workers in some privileged sectors of the economy (as well as the Communist Party leadership) benefited from separate systems for the distribution of goods and services. At the same time, ideological reasons precluded the abandonment of the stated political goal of a comprehensive health service. The unrealistic promise of services funded by totally inadequate resources created differences in access and quality, although these could be circumvented by informal connections (blat) and payments (Butler and Purchase 2004).

Stated objectives during the Soviet period and for several years afterwards were often treated as semi-propagandist slogans. Senior Russian medical professionals and officials would make statements during public presentations or in professional discussions about the need to improve the health of the population or elements within it, or to increase funding and improve quality. However, there were no attempts to define exactly what was meant or what was to be achieved. Russian health targets were far from the ideal set out in the SMART concept and contained little precision or specificity.

After the collapse of the Soviet Union there were a number of interesting attempts to develop more specific health objectives. A comprehensive set of targets was proposed in 1997 to develop health care and medical science over a five-year period, (Collegiums of the Ministry of Health 1997). Some other objectives were not announced explicitly as targets but were routinely monitored. For instance, infant mortality and tuberculosis incidence and mortality attracted considerable attention, even though they contributed a smaller share of the burden of diseases than noncommunicable disease in the adult population, which was seldom discussed (Lock et al. 2002). Most attempts to achieve change were only episodic and over long periods. The following section presents examples of initiatives to strengthen primary health care through the introduction of general practice/family medicine; to improve the demographic situation; and to create a system of health insurance that would generate additional funds and introduce better accountability.

Implementation of general practice: a failure of follow through

An attempt to introduce general practitioners (GPs) as a means of improving the performance of primary health care was one of the major failures of the Russian health system since the mid 1980s (Rese et al. 2005). The reallocation of available funds would have increased the numbers and skills of physicians trained but the implementation failed for purely political reasons.

Primary health care in the Russian Federation remains seriously understaffed. Since 1992, 2413 GPs have graduated from training centres, a negligible contribution to the approximately 100 000 required (of about 680 000 physicians employed by the Russian health-care system). Only 75% of those trained were employed in designated GP posts. Most graduates were based in traditional facilities with little support for new models of care. It is not clear how many were actually working as generalists because the system remains poorly defined with no incentives for broadening clinical scope. Internal documents from the Department of Human Resources and Education of the Ministry of Health indicate the dominance of the hospital sector in 2002 – 513 618 physicians in inpatient care; 204 888 in outpatient care. About half of the physicians in the outpatient sector were specialists, albeit with low levels of training and expertise in their specialist areas, so it was estimated that there were about 120 000 salaried positions for primary-contact physicians.

The number of generalists required seems large but the medical academies produce 25 000 physicians per year in the Russian Federation. With sufficient political will, it should not have taken long to reach the initial target of 100 000 GPs. In reality, efforts to introduce general practice underestimated the scale of the task and the resistance that would be faced. Although often very popular with patients, efforts to increase the numbers of GPs met strong opposition from the majority of other physicians. Paediatricians and other specialists who were most threatened by the results of the reform had very effective advocacy and lobbying tools. In contrast, supporters of the reform were not as influential. A third version of the legislation on general practice was launched in 2005 (Ministry of Health and Social Development 2005) and stimulated extensive debate. The decree had only a modest effect mainly because of corporate opposition from much of the medical community, most importantly by the medical elite of chief specialists and academicians.

Despite official backing to increase the numbers of GPs, there was insufficient investment to overcome resistance to change. There were no improvements in the legislative and regulatory framework or any development of an explicit human resource management policy. Staff motivation and retention was not addressed and the resources to support reform were not mobilized, neither was the support of municipalities and chief physicians who could facilitate the changes essential for success. Similar resistance to reforms prevented changes in medical student enrolment (see Box 11-1).

Box 11-1 *Medical student enrolment*

During the 1990s, the number of students accepted to medical education institutions dropped as a result of the economic situation in the country and as a result of pressure from the Ministry of Health and other parts of government, while the "overproduction crisis" seemed obvious. Student numbers fell slightly from 24 800 in 1990 to 24 700 in 1995 but increased to 35 000 in 2000. The rectors of the medical schools had much to lose from these unpopular reforms and so became powerful advocates against them. As a result, the number of physicians in the Russian Federation rose to 680 000 by the end of the 1990s. The ratio of 4.71 per 1000 population was significantly higher than in the EU (3.5 per 1000).

At the same time, the number of nurses consistently decreased from 1 844 000 to 1 611 700 in the last decade of the twentieth century. As a consequence, the ratio of nurses fell from 12.45 to 11.13 per 1000 people. The number of places in nursing education facilities steadily declined from 114 000 in 1990 to fewer than 83 000 in 2000. Unfortunately, nursing school directors could not exert sufficient influence despite the well-recognized undersupply of nurses.

Lack of ambition

One target of the Russian demographic policy launched in 2001 demonstrates that (in addition to opportunistic behaviour, cheating and creative accounting) there are situations where governments set targets which can be achieved without any extra effort.

When it became clear that the Russian Federation was facing a demographic crisis, three processes that contributed to this situation were considered (Government of the Russian Federation 2001). Falling birth rates were already well below the EU average; increasing mortality was well above the EU average; and migration created political concerns among radical politicians and some segments of the population. It was decided to concentrate on increasing birth rates, even though there was little evidence about how these could be changed.

The birth rate in the Russian Federation had declined since 1987 but was expected to rise in the early years of the 21st century. The small cohort born during the war years (1941–1945) reached peak child-bearing age during the 1960s. In turn they produced a relatively low number of children who reached child-bearing age during the 1990s. Social circumstances at the time of transition had contributed further to the low birth rate but the situation is projected to resolve itself by 2010.

Before the end of the Soviet Union, marriages traditionally took place at the age of 20 as young men sought to marry and start a family immediately after returning from compulsory military service. Significant social benefits (e.g. the possibility of receiving separate apartments or social welfare) acted as incentives for early childbearing in the absence of other legal opportunities to improve income but the social system started to fail even before the end of the Soviet Union. Additionally, the legalization of commerce in the late 1980s created previously unimaginable opportunities. The new economic reality often forced couples to postpone marriage until the age of 25–35 when they would have arranged separate accommodation, completed their education and carved out careers. Thus many couples postponed child bearing until their early 30s. The cohort produced by relatively high birth rates in the early 1980s reached child-bearing age in the late 1990s. This first generation to postpone families reached the age of 30 in 2002–2003.

In the late 1990s, insight into the underlying demographic process allowed the government to adopt policy targets which could not be influenced significantly by any interventions and required no action to achieve success and guarantee rewards. This also seemed very popular politically. Much later, a number of measures to stimulate reproduction were taken. From 2008, each mother receives the equivalent of US$ 10 000 on the third birthday of her second (and any subsequent) child. The money is earmarked for the child's education, to purchase property or invest in the mother's pension fund. Maternity-leave benefits were increased and obstetric certificates were introduced. These coupons are distributed to pregnant women to be exchanged for services provided by the antenatal centre, obstetric department and (from 2008) paediatric clinic. The continuous slow increase in birth rates since 1999 is a cause of major pride for the government which came into power a year later.

Defining health targets

Target setting in the Soviet Union was driven largely by communist ideology. As a result, targets had to be politically appropriate rather than relevant or necessary. This section discusses the communist ideology's influence on target setting and recent reforms to improve the organizational structure of health system policy-making in the Russian Federation.

Weak public health capacity

Currently, public health, epidemiology and demography are poorly established in the Russian Federation. The Soviet Union suppressed the sciences that address the determinants of disease and compare health indicators across countries and segments of the population. Such comparisons were considered dangerous as they might portray the Soviet economic system in a poor light by revealing unhealthy behaviours and poor population health relative to other industrialized countries. Scientific thought that was ideologically inconsistent with Marxism-Leninism was rejected, creating a markedly different model of science (with accompanying career paths and promotion criteria) (McKee 2007). Publications that set out research findings were evaluated differently in the Soviet Union – scientific merits were less important than ideological fidelity and the authors' membership of the Communist Party. Such membership also largely determined nominations for administrative positions. In the absence of peer-review processes and other forms of open debate the administrative tier largely determined what could be published. This situation persists in some institutions, albeit less formally.

The end of the Soviet Union brought many new opportunities in the commercial sector and few graduates chose a scientific career path. Also, Russian science was often associated with its Soviet ideological legacy. There was very little interaction between researchers and policy-makers. Politicians and officials perceived medicine as a complex science which they, as nonspecialists, could not understand. The absence of an evaluative culture ensured that there were few evaluations of interventions and policies on which to draw. Hence, issues concerning health outcomes and cost effectiveness were poorly understood among health professionals and the public. Clearly, any attempt to focus health targets on outcomes will require considerable strengthening of public health capacity in the Russian Federation.

Poor target definition

Management by objectives involves setting broad objectives and operationalizing them as specific targets, subtargets and indicators. Most of the outcome-related objectives of the Soviet system were broad and ambitious. Although many process indicators in other areas were consistent with the SMART concept, many health objectives established after the Second World War lacked coherence and were irrelevant to the goals being pursued. Furthermore, an objective could be SMART, feasible and detailed but would not be useful if it led in the wrong direction. The Communist Party promoted people on the basis of ideological conformity rather than scientific merit and often used advisers who possessed neither the skills nor the training necessary to produce relevant targets.

Typical examples of targets that were specific, measurable and time bound, but simply wrong, included the plan to reverse the flow of Siberian rivers (which did not occur), and to grow maize in cold areas of the Soviet Union, wheat in the north and cotton in the deserts of central Asia. These plans were suggested by senior party members and, due to the nature of the political system, could be debated only if this was instigated by someone more senior in the hierarchy. Irrelevant objectives were set in response to the increasing mortality from noncommunicable diseases. As public health and epidemiology were relatively underdeveloped in the Soviet Union, senior physicians and Communist Party officials produced targets consistent with the prevailing ideology. It was expected that population health would be improved by building more hospitals and training more doctors.

Organizational restructuring

There were limited efforts to reorganize the health system. This was not only due to lack of political support but also because health was not a priority in government policy-making. Targets were set but few were implemented. It remains unclear whether more recent administrative reforms will be implemented effectively.

There were some thoughts of restructuring health care after the end of the Soviet Union but most activities concentrated on the basic survival of the system. The Ministry of Health lost its role in developing secondary legislation and had few tools to implement its policies. Decrees produced by the Ministry tended to focus on relatively minor issues (such as reporting formats) and seldom reached the municipal facilities providing the bulk of care. The State Duma Committee on Health and Sports Affairs produced a number of laws, but these related more to social issues rather than the medical-care system. Health legislation was rather vague and influenced to some extent by lobby groups. This was true of anti-smoking legislation (Government of the Russian Federation 2001a) which included only those provisions considered acceptable by the tobacco industry (Danishevski and McKee 2002).

A comprehensive and ambitious set of targets was developed in the framework of the concept of development of health-care and medical science undertaken by the Collegiums of the Ministry of Health (Collegiums of the Ministry of Health 1997). Although approved by the Government of the Russian Federation at the end of 1997 and ratified by the legislature, this document remained peripheral to the general policy process. The Ministry of Health had no tools to even try to implement it, so it was soon forgotten and almost none of the targets were achieved. This was unfortunate as some were quite progressive, such as developing schools of public health or reforming the health-care financing system.

By 2004, the effects of the 1998 economic crisis had been mitigated by the increased income from higher oil prices. Following the presidential election, the President's administration initiated a radical overhaul of the system that posed questions about outcome-based assessment. Concrete indicators of progress became a popular overarching idea to guide reforms in all sectors, not only health. As part of this major administrative reform, the Ministries of Health, Social Affairs and Labour were merged in 2004 to create a new Ministry of Health and Social Development. The aim was to separate policy-formulation, policy-implementation and control functions. Thirteen former ministries and various other central bodies were abolished. These were replaced by 5 ministries that focused solely on policy development, 17 regulatory bodies to monitor adherence to policies in the regions and 20 agencies responsible for the delivery of services by federal institutions.

The new Ministry of Health and Social Development was given an enhanced policy-making role, set out in the draft strategy paper: *On improvement of structural efficiency of health care in Russia.* This was developed by the Centre for Strategic Development of the president's administration. The document was later rejected because many of the issues raised were considered controversial. These included a reduction in hospital capacity; strengthening primary health-care; management improvements; and the introduction of new systems of payment to facilities and individual providers of services.

Parliament considered other important pieces of legislation including one law on the reform of the health-insurance system and two on the legal basis of federal and municipal health-sector organizations. These two envisaged the creation of new legal entities – autonomous, not-for-profit specialized (medical) organizations. It was anticipated that this legislation would offer hospitals and primary-care organizations the scope to assume greater autonomy and (presumably) greater powers to rationalize facilities in line with changing health needs, linked to the creation of appropriate incentives.

In the light of the Russian Federation's previous experience of denationalizing state-owned assets, there are concerns that what is envisaged as autonomy will actually become privatization. There is little scope for competition because the centrally planned Soviet health-care system avoided duplication of facilities, except in a few large cities. There is a risk of creating private monopolies, with the potential to jeopardize access and damage quality of care.

A further problem is caused by Article 41 of the Russian Constitution which guarantees free health care to its citizens and specifies the legal status of organizations that can provide these services as state-run facilities. There are some concerns that any attempt to revise the status of medical facilities might undermine state guarantees of free care. Several Russian commentators have argued that the formal goals could have been achieved with relatively minor changes to budgetary law and that the current reforms reflect lobbying by the chief physicians in facilities with vested interests in supporting privatization. In addition, the reform process was subject to extensive lobbying from many constituencies, such as groups in the population seeking enhanced benefits and pharmaceutical companies seeking to have relatively ineffective medications included in approved drug lists.

Important questions about the role of the new merged ministry remain unanswered. Although formally responsible for policy development, the ministry's policy agenda is driven largely by outside interests. New legislation goes beyond the traditional focus on health-care delivery to include population health by setting goals to reduce mortality at working ages (especially by lowering rates of injuries and alcohol poisoning) as well as infant and maternal mortality. The new legislation also highlights the need for effective action against socially determined conditions such as drug addiction, smoking, hazardous drinking, sexually transmitted diseases, tuberculosis and AIDS. Whilst entirely laudable, these concerns seem to reflect the agenda of the presidential administration. There is anxiety about the national-security implications of the Russian Federation's high mortality, in particular because of fear about depopulation in some border areas. Priorities are announced in the president's annual speech but are not particularly detailed; the content of the National Priority Project on health is described below. With little evidence that the content of the new legislation reflects the concerns of the health ministry, it is unlikely to feel any sense of ownership (Danishevski and McKee 2005).

National Priority Project – Health. In 2005 the Russian Government approved four National Priority Projects: education, housing, agriculture and health. Despite very significant investment in the health-care system the latter project has not yielded much documentation. Initially discussed as a solution to the demographic crisis (with some emphasis on the need to reduce mortality) it eventually became a mechanism for infrastructure investment. Three initial objectives emerged – to develop primary health care; improve maternal and child health services; and develop high-technology medicine, although the last was not clearly defined. The current focus is the purchase of expensive equipment and ambulances. No clear health targets are set and the success of the project is reported according to the sums invested, rather than the outcomes achieved.

Another element is concerned with drugs provision. Recent reform of the pharmaceutical procurement mechanism created a system designed for those who are entitled to social protection – the Additional Drug Supply Program (DLO). Yet this system is unable to deliver the drugs needed by people with a wide variety of conditions. Often, those treated at primary-care level or those with serious chronic conditions requiring expensive treatment receive partial care or (at times) no care at all. The DLO has not solved the issue of equitable access to care for those treated on an inpatient or outpatient basis. Hospitalized patients are, at least formally, entitled to the provision of a full range of pharmaceuticals. Outpatients are supposed to purchase all the drugs they need, unless they are certified disabled. Such a system leads to perverse incentives for patients to be hospitalized and causes waste of scarce health-care resources. The associations of patients with epilepsy and haemophilia argue that there was an improvement in mortality among their members but this was not monitored properly. It should also be mentioned that the system is very unpopular and seems not to have functioned adequately, at least in its early stages.

Exerting influence

Recent administrative reforms to reorganize the governance structures that link local authorities and federal bodies were intended to centralize control, improve coordination and provide effective mechanisms for exerting federal influence at the local level. This section discusses the current systems and the planned reforms.

The 1993 Russian Constitution established the regions as 89 equal subjects of the Russian Federation, led by elected governments within a federal structure. This process was encouraged by western advisers who saw the strengthened regions as a counterweight to the federal government. Each of the regions was divided into between 30 and 100 municipalities, with elected executive and legislative branches of government. These municipalities are small and supposedly have limited influence over most major political decisions but their influence on health care can hardly be overstated. Municipalities emerged from the 1993 Constitution as important bodies as they owned the facilities in which most of the routine health care was delivered. Moreover, they provided a substantial amount of health-care financing as they were responsible for insurance contributions for the non-working population.

The federal government was often unable to intervene directly in municipal affairs, as they fell within the responsibility of regional authorities. However, the municipalities had considerable autonomy. For instance, those municipalities that were net contributors (from their taxes) to the regional budget largely oversaw their own operations. Even the poor and financially dependent municipalities had weak lines of accountability that involved only the head of that municipality and the regional governor. The head of the regional health authority did not have the power to close beds in municipal hospitals or to employ financial sanctions even if the municipalities disregarded regional or federal guidelines. A weak accountability mechanism pushed the government towards a higher degree of centralization.

In May 2000, President Putin issued a decree that replaced the previous structure of nine supra-regional economic groupings with seven federal regions (Government of the Russian Federation 2000). He appointed his own representatives to lead them, giving them wide-ranging but poorly defined authority. Although the new regions had no formal responsibility for the health sector, the President's representatives soon appointed deputies to fill a perceived vacuum in relation to health and other policy areas. This precipitated an unforeseen process of interregional coordination within the health sector. Effective since 2005 (accepted by the federal parliament in December 2004), the new legislation authorizes the President to approve the appointment of regional governors to the regional parliaments. This strengthens the means to exert centralized control, making supra-regional arrangements less important for management but still important for oversight and control. In addition, several regions merged in 2004 and reduced the number of subjects of the Russian Federation to 87.

The administrative reform granted the new Ministry of Health and Social Development an enhanced policy-making role but removed many of its traditional functions, such as the management of federal bodies (including research institutes, medical schools and tertiary referral facilities) as well as regulation and epidemiological surveillance. A new Federal Agency for Health Care and Social Development assumed responsibility for funding and managing federal bodies that undertake research and clinical care, and for medical education. Moreover, another new organization (The Service) assumed the regulatory functions to oversee the work of all health- and social-care providers in the regions.

A new body, the Federal Service for Supervision of Consumer Protection and Human Welfare, performs sanitary and epidemiological surveillance (SES) functions based in part on the existing network of sanitary epidemiological facilities that were concerned traditionally with monitoring food, water, and occupational safety (President of the Russian Federation 2004). The two Services were intended to become the major instruments for exerting influence and controlling the implementation of the new ministry's policies at regional and local levels. It is quite probable that these organizations will use their rights to introduce financial sanctions, with legal action against extreme divergence from official policy. However, after three years of reform, the function of the Service supervising healthcare remains less than clear.

Changes introduced in these administrative reforms can be expected to assist the federal government to exert its influence but it is unclear whether the new ministry will be able to carry out policy development more effectively. Currently, the presidential administration largely drives the policy agenda so the means of exerting influence seems to be nearly as hierarchical as in Soviet times and ownership is not devolved to the regional and municipal levels. Furthermore, it remains to be seen whether the health ministry will formulate effective targets when it defines the strategies to implement the reforms in detail.

Collecting and using intelligence

Any centrally planned system requires appropriate mechanisms to collect, analyse and distribute information relevant to the objectives being pursued. None of these was fully achieved in the Soviet health-care system, partly due to the incredible volume of information that the system required but mainly because of ideological barriers to effective and responsive management.

The central planning system required large systems of data collection to be developed. Even almost two decades after the end of the Soviet Union, up to 30 000 health-care indicators are requested from regions. However, all of these are at an aggregate level, often unreliable, easily modified and with little validation. It is important to note that the extensive system for monitoring health and health care in the Soviet Union has changed little in the Russian Federation. It remains more closely aligned with the needs of the defunct command system rather than the needs of those seeking to monitor progress on targets. Although the information collected could generate aggregate statistical data rapidly in a standardized format, the validity and value of some data were relatively low. For instance, statistics on the provision of antenatal care and skilled birth attendants yielded figures similar to those in the EU but could not explain the poor perinatal outcomes and high maternal mortality (Parkhurst et al. 2005). This problem was exacerbated by an almost complete lack of population health research.

There are several examples of when results obtained from the monitoring system did not satisfy the communist hierarchy during the Soviet period. When this occurred, data were withheld from academics, scientists and administrators, e.g. data on declining life expectancy during the late 1960s were not made publicly available until about three decades later. A tendency to modify definitions and even to manipulate statistics as a means of propaganda only exacerbated this situation, and is still the case for infant mortality (for example, Danishevski et al. 2005).

The data-gathering system served the ideological needs and private interests of senior civil servants and politicians but, as a result, was detrimental to staff morale. Employees at all three levels of the state system (local facilities, regional health authorities and the Ministry of Health) provided data to the State Committee for Statistics (Goskomstat) but the information was commonly believed to be unreliable and of little value. Limited capacity in epidemiology often leads to poor or irrelevant presentation of data. Even when the information is passed on to decision-makers, they are seldom able to use it. Official channels for providing information to decision-makers do not work well and many statistical reports remain on the shelves of the statistical agencies.

Many new data-collection systems were created to reflect changing needs after the end of the Soviet Union. However, these often duplicated older systems that remained in place and were seldom able to provide data of greater validity. The same statistics clerk was responsible for data collection and accountable to the head of the medical facility and must balance the interests of the employer against the needs of the centre.

Beginning in 2004, administrative reporting included an idea to shift towards performance-based reimbursement. A number of committees were established to develop monitoring indicators that could be used as a basis for funding decisions. While the attempt was soon abandoned, in view of the already strong incentives for underreporting or inaccurate reporting, the introduction of financial incentives might not have led to better data. This raises questions about the relevance of target setting in this environment and how incentives could be aligned to encourage accurate reporting.

Lessons learned

The challenges of using targets in the Russian Federation must be interpreted in the light of the Soviet legacy. The history of target use stretches over many decades, yet contains many negative lessons as ideology pervaded government policy to create perverse incentives and a lack of objective assessment. While recognizing this negative experience, it is important not to discard the idea of targets but rather to recognize the importance of taking account of context (Hunter 1999).

Targets in the health sector in the Soviet Union (and later in the Russian Federation) have evolved unsteadily. The first target to achieve universal health-care coverage was followed by efforts to tackle the rising tide of non-communicable diseases, increase health-care funding and, more recently, develop a culture of management by objectives that converged in the National Priority Project on health. Yet throughout this period, and at least until 2005, health was seldom high on the agenda and has not been a priority. Most targets were broadly defined, focused on expanding the infrastructure and almost never outcome oriented. Furthermore, an almost complete lack of public health professionals and epidemiologists (and a very limited pool of demographers) in the Russian Federation made it almost impossible to develop and monitor targets. The lack of capacity led to unrealistic targets. For example, in 2005 it was suggested that change in life expectancy should be used as a short-term measure of performance, while later the birth rate was considered to be an indicator of health.

Furthermore, the lack of an independent data-collection system can give rise to unreliable data. In the health-care system there is a clear need for statistics clerks to operate independently from the heads of medical facilities. Employment at regional level, rather than by municipal hospitals, would help to remove some of the conflicts of interest in data collection. Further, extensive field testing and research to assess current data needs should be used as the basis to replace obsolete data-collection systems. However, this will achieve little until health becomes a better defined and higher priority in the Russian Federation (Marquez et al. 2007).

REFERENCES

Andreev EM et al. (2003). The evolving pattern of avoidable mortality in Russia. *International Journal of Epidemiology,* 32(3):437-446.

Butler B, Purchase S (2004). Personal networking in Russian post Soviet life. *Research and Practice in Human Resource Management,* 12(1):34-60.

Collegiums of the Ministry of Health (1997). *Concept of development of healthcare and medical science.* Moscow, Government of Russian Federation.

Danishevski K, McKee M (2002). Campaigners fear that Russia's new tobacco law won't work. *BMJ,* 324(7334):382.

Danishevski K, McKee M (2005). Reforming the Russian health-care system. *Lancet,* 365(9464):1012-1014.

Danishevski K et al. (2005). Inequalities in birth outcomes in Russia: evidence from Tula oblast. *Paediatr Perinat Epidemiol,* 19(5):352-359.

Drucker PF (1954). *Practice of management.* New York, Harper.

Field MG (1957). *Doctor and patient in Soviet Russia.* Cambridge, MA, Harvard University Press.

Field MG (1999). Reflections on a painful transition: from socialized to insurance medicine in Russia. *Croatian Medical Journal,* 40(2):202-209.

Government of the Russian Federation (2000). *Decree on "improving efficiency of Presidential administration to fulfil constitutional duties". N849.* Moscow, Government of the Russian Federation.

Government of the Russian Federation (2001). *Concept of demographic development of Russian Federation in the period up to 2015.* Moscow, Government of the Russian Federation.

Government of the Russian Federation (2001a). *The law on limiting tobacco smoking.* Moscow, Government of the Russian Federation.

Hunter DJ (1999). Implementing health targets in health care. *Eurohealth,* 5(3):9-11.

Lock K et al. (2002). What targets for international development policies are appropriate for improving health in Russia? *Health Policy Plan,* 17(3):257-263.

Marquez P et al. (2007). Adult health in the Russian Federation: more than just a health problem. *Health Aff (Millwood),* 26(4):1040-1051.

McKee M (2007). Cochrane on communism: the influence of ideology on the search for evidence. *Int J Epidemiol,* 36(2):269-273.

Ministry of Health and Social Development (2005). *Decree on the order of implementation of activities by general practitioner (family doctor).* Moscow, Ministry of Health and Social Development.

Omran AR (1971). The epidemiologic transition. A theory of the epidemiology of population change. *Milbank Mem Fund Q,* 49(4):509-538.

Parkhurst JO, Danischevski K, Balabanova D (2005). International maternal health indicators and middle-income countries: Russia. *BMJ,* 331(7515):510-513.

President of the Russian Federation (2004). *Decree on system and structure of federal organs of executive government N314 of 9 March 2004.* Moscow, Government of the Russian Federation.

Rese A et al. (2005). Implementing general practice in Russia: getting beyond the first steps. *BMJ,* 331(7510):204-207.

Tulchinsky TH, Varavikova EA (1996). Addressing the epidemiologic transition in the former Soviet Union: strategies for health system and public health reform in Russia. *Am J Public Health,* 86(3):313-320.